Computer Games and Language Learning

Palgrave Macmillan's Digital Education and Learning

Much has been written during the first decade of the new millennium about the potential of digital technologies to produce a transformation of education. Digital technologies are portrayed as tools that will enhance learner collaboration and motivation, and develop new multimodal literacy skills. Accompanying this has been the move from understanding literacy on the cognitive level to an appreciation of the sociocultural forces shaping learner development. Responding to these claims, the Digital Education and Learning Series explores the pedagogical potential and realities of digital technologies in a wide range of disciplinary contexts across the educational spectrum both in and outside of class. Focusing on local and global perspectives, the series responds to the shifting landscape of education, the way digital technologies are being used in different educational and cultural contexts, and examines the differences that lie behind the generalizations of the digital age. Incorporating cutting-edge volumes with theoretical perspectives and case studies (single authored and edited collections), the series provides an accessible and valuable resource for academic researchers, teacher trainers, administrators, and students interested in interdisciplinary studies of education and new and emerging technologies.

Series Editors:

Michael Thomas is senior lecturer at the University of Central Lancashire and editor in chief of the *International Journal of Virtual and Personal Learning Environments* (IJVPLE).

James Paul Gee is a Mary Lou Fulton Presidential Professor at Arizona State University. His most recent book is *Policy Brief: Getting Over the Slump: Innovation Strategies to Promote Children's Learning* (2008).

John Palfrey is the head of school at Phillips Academy, Andover, and a senior research fellow at the Berkman Center for Internet & Society at Harvard. He is coauthor of *Born Digital: Understanding the First Generation of Digital Natives* (2008).

Digital Education
Edited by Michael Thomas

Digital Media and Learner Identity: The New Curatorship
By John Potter

Rhetoric/Composition/Play through Video Games: Reshaping Theory and Practice of Writing
Edited by Richard Colby, Matthew S. S. Johnson, and Rebekah Shultz Colby

Computer Games and Language Learning
By Mark Peterson

Computer Games and Language Learning

Mark Peterson

COMPUTER GAMES AND LANGUAGE LEARNING
Copyright © Mark Peterson, 2013.

Softcover reprint of the hardcover 1st edition 2013 978-1-137-00516-8

First published in 2013 by
PALGRAVE MACMILLAN®
in the United States—a division of St. Martin's Press LLC,
175 Fifth Avenue, New York, NY 10010.

Where this book is distributed in the UK, Europe and the rest of the world,
this is by Palgrave Macmillan, a division of Macmillan Publishers Limited,
registered in England, company number 785998, of Houndmills,
Basingstoke, Hampshire RG21 6XS.

Palgrave Macmillan is the global academic imprint of the above companies
and has companies and representatives throughout the world.

Palgrave® and Macmillan® are registered trademarks in the United States,
the United Kingdom, Europe and other countries.

ISBN 978-1-349-43465-7   ISBN 978-1-137-00517-5 (eBook)

DOI 10.1057/9781137005175

Library of Congress Cataloging-in-Publication Data

Peterson, Mark, 1965–
        Computer games and language learning / Mark Peterson.
             pages cm.—(Digital Education and Learning)
        Includes bibliographical references and index.

        1. Language and languages—Study and teaching—Technological
innovations. 2. Computer-assisted instruction. 3. Video games—Study
and teaching. 4. Computer games. 5. Educational technology. I. Title.

P53.855.P48 2013
410.285—dc23   2013008732

A catalogue record of the book is available from the British Library.

Design by Newgen Knowledge Works (P) Ltd., Chennai, India.

First edition: August 2013

10 9 8 7 6 5 4 3 2 1

For my grandfather Alexander "Alec" Toshney
San Fairy Ann

Contents

Tables

Series Foreword: Language, Learning, and Games

The human mind learns through experience, especially experiences where a person has an action to take whose outcome really matters to the person. Language is a tool for social and individual problem solving and it is our most crucial human tool for taking action in the world and learning from experience. Succinctly put, this is a statement of an "embodied" view of cognition and a "social and situated" view of language. Words do not primarily or originally get their meanings from other words ("definitions"), but from images and actions from our experiences in the world. If I say "The coffee spilled, go get a mop," this remark gets and gives meaning to the world quite differently than "The coffee spilled, go get a broom" or "The coffee spilled, go stack it again." Words like "honor" require experiences with codes of honor in the world. Words get meaning from experience, differently in different contexts, and then help organize and regiment our experiences of the world in turn.

On this view all learning is a form of language learning. Different "registers" of language (or different "social languages") mediate the relationship between language and experience differently in different domains. The language of physics, of video games, of intimacy, and many more, are formed from and form our experience in different areas. Thus, it is odd how in formal education cognition is so often cut off from language (as in a science class where language is treated as a transparent window onto thought and the world and not a force in its own right). It is odd, as well, how often in school we give people texts and textbooks, but no experiences in the world beyond reading words. This is rather like trying to understand a video game by reading the manual, but never really playing the game. Worse, since it is the game that gives meaning originally to the words of the manual, it is better to do (act) first (often with interactive dialogue to mentor the experience) and read second, so the words can then meaningfully help organize, regiment, and improve our learning from experience as we begin to play the game more critically and reflectively.

Learning a language like English or Spanish, or a social language like the language of physics or civics, is hard to do in the isolation of the four walls in a classroom. Furthermore, such isolation privileges those who have already had relevant experiences outside the classroom and have already thereby begun an authentic process of language development. But sometimes it is hard to marry words and the world. We humans cannot be electrons and so cannot really experience anything—other than imaginatively—from their perspectives. We cannot send every student to Spain or Mexico or set them up with fluent Spanish-speaking friends and colleagues to work on action and dialogue in the world in Spanish with them. Here is where video games and related digital technologies come in. As goal-driven simulations where players have to take action and often today engage socially with others, video games are a promising platform for getting out of the isolation of the classroom and showing learners how to marry words, thoughts, actions, and goals that matter to them. In a game you can be an electron. In a game, you can engage in joint problem solving in Spanish with Spanish speakers and mentors. Games are a promising platform for embodying learning and situating meaning in rich virtual worlds and rich social spaces built around them.

The area of video games and language learning is a relatively new, but fast-moving one. As our technologies improve (e.g., for voice and face recognition) the area will, I am confident, become transformative for the future of language learning, which is to say, for learning as a whole. Mark Peterson's *Computer Games and Language Learning* is your best current field guide to this new and exciting area.

Series Editors
James P. Gee
Mary Lou Fulton Presidential
Professor of Literacy Studies
Arizona State University

Michael Thomas
Senior Lecturer in Language Learning Technologies
University of Central Lancashire

John Palfrey
Head of School
Phillips Academy, Andover

Preface

Digital technologies are greatly influencing all spheres of education, and the field of language education is no exception. These technologies now form an integral part of many foreign language programs. The dramatic growth of the Internet has enabled individual language learners to access, both inside and outside of the classroom, an ever-expanding array of software programs, communication devices, and online resources. Language educators are increasingly using these tools as a means to facilitate language learning. This book focuses on an important aspect of this phenomenon—the use of computer games. The investigation ultimately aims to answer the following questions: Is participation in computer gaming beneficial for language learners? Does computer gaming represent, as has been claimed in relation to other spheres, a paradigm shift in language education? These questions are of great relevance at present, as while technology advances rapidly and computer gaming continues to expand globally, it has not made a significant impact on mainstream language education. Despite claims made regarding the value of participation in computer gaming in educational research, its use in the field of computer-assisted language learning (henceforth CALL) remains limited. Moreover, as the discussion will show, although there is increasing interest in the use of computer games, the gameplay of language learners has yet to be subject to the kind of extensive research found in other areas. This book represents an attempt to answer the above questions. In order to provide background, the initial discussion revisits the history of the application of technological innovations in CALL. This is followed by an overview of game theories and the genres that have been used in CALL. The discussion explores theoretical rationales for the use of computer gaming in education that draw on relevant theories of human learning. This is followed by an examination of contemporary theories of second language acquisition (henceforth SLA). Rationales for the use of computer games in CALL that draw on constructs proposed in these theories are examined. The discussion then focuses on providing a critical overview of both early and more recent research on the use of computer games in CALL. Previous work is explored in-depth, in an effort to avoid the well-documented tendency in CALL research to neglect prior work when utilizing new developments in computer technology. As gaming continues to evolve and research work expands, I am aware that the discussion of research will inevitably represent something of a snapshot. However, as has been noted elsewhere, there are many valuable insights to be gained from looking back to early and more recent research, not least as a means to guide work in the future. As this effort reveals the urgent need for more research focusing on learner interaction during gameplay, this book further contains an analysis of findings drawn from a case study. This provides important new insights into the potential of network-based role-playing games and the challenges inherent in undertaking learner-based CALL projects involving the use of such games. The conclusion summarizes key findings and identifies a number of areas that may prove valuable in future research.

Chapter 1 provides a context for the remainder of the discussion. As noted above, the questions pursued inevitably require a critical examination of the past use of new technologies in CALL. The discussion in this chapter highlights the history of three major technological innovations in CALL and examines what I term as the *false dawn phenomenon*: the belief that the latest new technological development will inevitably revolutionize learning. In the discussion, attention is drawn to the persistence of barriers to technology implementation in formal educational contexts and the limitations of CALL research. The case is made that if CALL is to develop as a field, then theories of language acquisition must play a central role in guiding research and development. This discussion will, it is hoped, alert the reader to the dangers inherent in technocentric thinking and encourage a more balanced view of the potential of computer gaming in language education.

Chapter 2 begins by providing an overview of influential definitions of play and computer gaming proposed in the literature. The discussion examines computer game theories, and then explores key design elements and features of computer games, focusing on the particular genres that have been identified in research as having potential as tools for language learning. The discussion provides a description and overview of game types that will be examined in later chapters. In order to provide a context to better comprehend the educational potential of computer games, chapter 3 explores influential rationales proposed for the use of digital games in education. In this context, relevant theories from computer gaming research are examined, as new conceptions of literacy and perspectives on the use of digital media that have become increasingly influential in education research. Chapter 4 continues the exploration of rationales by providing an overview of the particular SLA theories that have been proposed to justify the use of certain types of computer games in CALL. The discussion focuses on constructs drawn from theories of language learning proposed in both cognitive and social accounts of SLA. I observe that insights from both these perspectives are valuable, as they can inform a comprehensive and credible conceptual framework to guide future research.

Chapter 5 investigates early research on the use of computer games in CALL. The discussion shows that the use of computer games does not, as is sometimes supposed, represent a new phenomenon. This chapter revisits early pioneering work in order to provide a context for the discussion in the following chapter. Chapter 6 focuses on providing an analysis of significant findings drawn from studies and projects that are illustrative of more recent research. The critical overview conducted in this chapter draws attention to some promising preliminary findings and also emphasizes a number of issues that require investigation in future research. In the discussion in chapter 7, the need for additional research is emphasized. This chapter further provides an analysis of the key findings of a case study involving the use by undergraduate EFL learners based in Japan of one particularly promising genre of computer game that has been the subject of only limited research—a massively multiplayer online role-playing game (henceforth MMORPG). The analysis highlights the challenges inherent in undertaking learner-based research on the use of network-based computer games in CALL. The discussion draws attention to a number of positive findings and also emphasizes important issues that have been identified in previous research. Chapter 8 concludes the discussion by providing answers to the questions set out in the preface. The discussion in this chapter revisits significant findings and issues raised in this book. I draw attention to the broadly encouraging results of previous research and argue that additional work is urgently needed. The case is made for a balanced approach to future research and development work that acknowledges and builds on the results of prior work. I argue that in order to avoid the problems inherent in technology-led development work, there is a need for systematic theory-led research that recognizes both the potential benefits and issues associated with the use of computer games in CALL. The chapter then examines some noteworthy contemporary projects that exemplify this approach. The discussion concludes by identifying a number of areas with potential in future research.[1]

---

[1] A variety of terms such as *video games* and *digital games* are used in the literature to describe computer-based games. Following Sundqvist and Sylvén (2012, 189), the term *computer games* is adopted in this book to describe games played on computers, mobile communication devices, and consoles.

Acknowledgments

I would like to thank the many people who have assisted in making this book a reality. Thanks are due to friends whose ideas, feedback, and encouragement have contributed to the completion of this book including Michal Thomas, Bernard Susser, and Alex Gilmore. I would like to express my gratitude to the students who participated in the research included in this book and to the many students and colleagues who have collaborated with me over the years. I also thank my parents Stella and Adam, and my sisters Lisa, Maria, Angela, and their families. Finally, I would like to express my thanks to Mari and Kyle for their understanding and support.

MARK PETERSON
Kyoto, October 2012

Acknowledgements

CHAPTER 1

CALL and New Digital Technologies

Assimilating New Computer Technologies in CALL: An Overview

Innovations in computer technology have a history of use in language education dating back over five decades (Davies 2007; Kerth 1995). Davies (1997, 27) observes that computers and computer-based technologies have been in use in language education since the 1960s. The early uses of computer technologies were influenced by the computer-assisted instruction (henceforth CAI) movement, and development continued with the eventual emergence of CALL in the 1980s. In order to obtain a broad perspective on the potential of computer gaming in language education, an examination of how three significant developments in computer technology were applied in the past is instructive, as it provides valuable insights that are highly relevant to the needs of the present.

Mainframe Computers

The development of commercial mainframe computers in the 1950s led to interest from educational researchers in using their capacities as instructional tools. One of the first attempts to use a mainframe-based computer system in education was the PLATO (Programmed Logic for Automated Teaching Operations) system initiated at the University of Illinois in 1960. As the name suggests, this system was grounded in the behaviorist view of CAI dominant at the time. PLATO made use of mainframe computers connected to multilingual student terminals, and was designed to provide self-paced programmed instruction in a variety of fields for large numbers of students (Butler-Pascoe 2011). The system incorporated a number of novel features including a touch screen that displayed graphics (Ariew 1974) and an early form of email that enabled individual users to communicate with each other in real time through the use of typed text. Moreover, PLATO provided access to audio, on-screen help, and an advanced management system. This was designed to facilitate monitoring and record keeping of student performance (Chapelle and Jamieson 1981). The system utilized a programming language known as TUTOR that enabled teachers to participate in materials development. In language education, PLATO was used to provide a variety of language-learning activities that drew on audiolingualism. Typical activities included multiple choice–based grammar and vocabulary drills, tutorials, and translation tests. The technologies provided were advanced for the time, and the system was seen as a highly promising tool for foreign language education (Grundlehner 1974; Hart 1981). The use of PLATO to teach a variety of languages generated a high degree of interest and expectation in the CALL research community (Hart 1995, 17). Researchers investigated the use of the system in a number of learner-based projects (Beatty 2003). Work focused on the use of PLATO in Russian (Curtin et al. 1972), German (Grundlehner 1974), and French courses (Marty 1981, 1982). The above researchers claimed that the system offered a number of advantages including self-paced individualized practice, feedback, reduced anxiety, and enhanced motivation. However, limitations of the system soon became apparent. The need for learner training and hardware limitations were identified as issues, as was the presence of negative teacher attitudes toward the system (Grundlehner 1974). These factors, and high development costs, represented barriers to use (Marty 1982).

Over the years of its operation, the PLATO system generated a sizeable database of instructional materials covering a variety of foreign languages. As Hart (1995, 35) points out, elements of the system foreshadowed later multimedia technologies. As Levy observes (1997, 17) although subject to limitations, PLATO was an innovative project and represented one of the first attempts to use new computer technologies in language education on a large scale and in a sustained manner. However, the early promise of the system was not followed up. Federal funding was withdrawn, and this factor coupled with high development costs (Ahmad et al. 1985), licensing issues (R. Sanders 1995), and a general reaction among language educators against programmed learning (Salaberry 2001), led development work to be curtailed. These issues, and the rapid pace of technological change, resulted in a situation where the original PLATO system is now no longer under active development.

Multimedia CD-ROMs

The emergence of microcomputers in the late 1970s stimulated new developments in language-learning software. As most early microcomputers lacked audio and video, programs of the time were largely designed around text-based activities (Higgins and Johns 1984). However, by the 1980s, technology had advanced to the stage where personal computers incorporating CD-ROM drives, sound cards, and video-playing capabilities had made their appearance. These developments, coupled with advances in digital storage technologies, prompted the creation of multimedia CD-ROMs designed specifically for use in language education. These combined text-based learning activities with access to high quality audio, visually appealing color graphics, and video. They further provided a higher degree of interactivity than early programs through the provision of hypertext and more user-friendly interfaces (Iwabuchi and Fotos 2004). The emergence of multimedia CD-ROMs occurred at a time when new views of computer-based learning had become increasingly influential. These views came to be identified with the concept of CALL. This concept emphasized a move away from drills to more creative and engaging uses of computers (Philips 1987). Multimedia CD-ROMs were perceived as tools with great potential by CALL researchers (Watts 1997; Woodbury 1998) as they offered exposure to comprehensible input, and immediate feedback—factors identified as playing an important role in language learning in SLA research (Krashen 1985; Long 1985). Self-contained CD-ROMs incorporating multimedia activities were perceived as useful tools for the support of individualized learning and the development of learner autonomy as they encourage learners to take responsibility for their own learning (Brett 1998). Moreover, by presenting a wide range of authentic materials in an accessible manner, multimedia CD-ROMs represented an advance over the simple text-based activities of the mainframe era and as such appeared to provide enhanced opportunities for language learning (Hagen 1995). As multimedia technologies continued to evolve, large numbers of CALL CD-ROMs were produced particularly during the 1990s. This phenomenon led researchers to examine the use of multimedia CD-ROMs in learner-based studies. A number of beneficial aspects of the use of multimedia CD-ROMs in CALL are reported in the literature. Research has shown CD-ROMs that provide annotations may enhance retention of new vocabulary (Chun and Plass 1996). Studies indicate that the use of CD-ROMs may enhance listening comprehension (Brett 1997) and improve grammar knowledge (Felix 2000). Researchers further draw attention to positive attitudes and enhanced motivation (Fleta et al. 1999).

As the above discussion shows, the potential of multimedia CD-ROMs is recognized in the CALL literature. However, the limitations of this technology have been the focus of discussion. A number of recurrent issues have been identified. Hlas and Vuksanovich (2007) explored teacher beliefs regarding the use of Spanish CD-ROMs in elementary schools in the United States. They claimed, on the basis of their findings, that many teachers did not make regular use of CD-ROMs in their classes as the products available were frequently perceived as being of poor quality and did not meet teacher needs (Hlas and Vuksanovich 2007, 775). They identified a lack of communication between educators and publishing companies as the main reason for resistance to CD-ROM use. The closed nature of many CD-ROMs where the content cannot be modified to meet the needs of specific learner groups was viewed as a major drawback (Chambers and Bax 2006, 475). The costs and long lead times necessary for the developing of high quality content are seen as limitations (Brett and Nash 1999, 19), as is the variable nature of product quality (Eastment 1996). The development of robust, widely accepted evaluation criteria is an important issue that remains unresolved (Murray and Barnes 1998). The limited nature of research on the use of multimedia in CALL has also been viewed as problematic (Plass and Jones 2005). Since the late 1990s, concerns had been raised regarding the limited influence of SLA research findings on the design of many multimedia-based learning activities (Chapelle 1998). In this context, the commercially driven nature of much CD-ROM development has been viewed with concern (Warschauer 1996, 8). The literature draws attention to the fact that while innovative work has been undertaken (Blake 1999), the activities in many CD-ROMs continue to revolve around language drills (Davies 2007), and do not provide opportunities for the communicative interaction and negotiation of meaning that are held to play an important role in SLA. Davies (1997, 33) observes that technical barriers and equipment availability still hamper large-scale CD-ROM use in many educational institutions. This researcher emphasizes that although CD-ROMs have long been viewed as representing a technology with potential in CALL, this potential has all too often not been fully realized. Although development work on multimedia use in CALL continues (Sydorenko 2010), this technology has now been superseded by Internet-based learning activities (Davies 2007).

Videoconferencing

The emergence of the Internet and World Wide Web in the 1990s represented a major advance in computer technologies and marked the beginning of a new era of development in CALL. For the first time, language educators had access to a range of accessible communication tools that enabled both synchronous and asynchronous communication over distance. Computer-mediated communication (henceforth CMC) was seen as a development with major implications (Warschauer and Kern 2000). The obvious potential of these tools to reduce traditional constraints on learning such as time and distance led to claims that network-based communication technologies would revolutionize language education (Warschauer, Turbee, and Roberts 1996). Of these new innovations, videoconferencing appeared particularly promising (Andrews 1994; Wang 2004; Zähner, Fauverge, and Wong 2000). By bringing together real-time communication technologies such as video, text chat, and interactive whiteboards, these tools offered a means to overcome a major drawback that had been identified in multimedia CD-ROMs, namely, the absence of meaningful communicative interaction (Hampel 2003). Videoconferencing provides exposure not only to comprehensible input from peers, but also opportunities to engage in negotiation of meaning (Gass and Varonis 1994) involving the production of comprehensible target language (henceforth TL), a process that is claimed to support acquisition by raising learner awareness (Swain 1985). This technology facilitates international projects where learners have access to diverse groups of peers and native speakers located overseas, providing opportunities to develop communicative competence and intercultural knowledge (O'Dowd 2000). From the mid 1990s onward researchers and practitioners were quick to explore the use of conferencing tools that utilized real-time video communication in a range of studies. A number of benefits of participation in videoconferencing are identified in the literature. Researchers claim that videoconferencing is enjoyable, may increase learner confidence and motivation (McAndrew, Foubister, and Mayes 1996). Research indicates that the use of this technology may support active collaboration involving TL dialogue (Wong and Fauverge 1999) and in the case of international projects enhances knowledge of the TL culture (O'Dowd 2000). There is also limited evidence that negotiation of meaning occurs (Wang 2006).

The literature on the use of videoconferencing in CALL, while acknowledging possible benefits, draws attention to a number of issues associated with its use. Development costs, advanced hardware, and network infrastructure requirements are identified as potential barriers to use (Hampel 2003; Perkins 1999). Although advances in technology have reduced costs in recent years (Ciekanski and Chanier 2008), training and support needs remain significant constraints that act to restrict the widespread implementation of videoconferencing in many language programs (Wang 2004). Though reliability is improving, videoconferencing remains a technology that is challenging to implement in many educational institutions. The online nature of the communication in videoconferencing where there can be delays between messages due to bandwidth issues and the accompanying reduction in communication cues can lead to difficulties (Hampel 2003, 30). These factors have been identified as having the potential to hamper group discussion (Goodfellow et al. 1996). User errors caused by limited computer skills and difficulties managing multimodal interfaces represent additional problems (Hampel and Hauck 2004). The limited nature of the research in this area compared to other types of CMC is noteworthy (Wang 2004). Although research continues (Jauregi and Bañados 2008) the majority of studies suggest that due to the considerable logistical and technical difficulties encountered in implementing large-scale projects, video conferencing is a tool best utilized for small group interaction and individual tutoring (Buckett, Stringer, and Datta 1999; O'Dowd 2000).

Assimilating New Technologies in CALL: Opportunities and Issues

The prior discussion has shown that advances in computer technologies have stimulated a wide range of projects and research work. In examining this work, a number of recurrent themes become apparent. The following discussion focuses on exploring these themes in greater detail.

False Dawn Phenomenon

A noteworthy feature of the application of new computer technologies in CALL is the repeated tendency to view each new innovation as a potential breakthrough when it emerges (Kohn 1995; Warschauer, Turbee, and Roberts 1996). This trend is frequently accompanied by the appearance of sweeping claims that are made on the basis of rather limited evidence (Biber 1992; Huh and Hu 2005). Although there are researchers who advocate a more cautious approach (Chapelle 1997; Davies 2007), this phenomenon nonetheless remains a striking feature of the literature down to the present and demonstrates the pervasive influence of the belief that technological advances are in themselves beneficial (Stockwell 2007). As was observed previously, the PLATO project was seen initially as highly significant. However, promising development work was not continued as the system was overtaken by technological change. Multimedia CD-ROMs and videoconferencing tools are further examples of technologies that were perceived as significant innovations when they first emerged. This discussion emphasizes that although some valuable research work has been conducted that draws attention to the potential of these technologies, there has been at best only limited follow-up. Indeed the above technologies, though still in use, are now regarded as either largely obsolete or occupying only niche areas. As Davies (1997, 2007) has warned repeatedly, technocentric thinking remains influential. This situation has acted to restrain the development of a balanced and critical approach to the assimilation of new technologies that is necessary for systematic and effective development in CALL. There is a need to move beyond the wow factor (Murray and Barnes 1998) if innovations with potential, such as computer games, are to be implemented and researched effectively in the future.

The Persistence of Barriers to Effective Technology Implementation

This discussion draws attention to another factor that is often overlooked in the literature, namely, the persistence of barriers to the effective application of technological advances in CALL (Levy and Stockwell 2006). The issue of funding was noted in the discussion of the PLATO project. The general absence of sustained funding in many institutions contributes to a situation where large-scale projects are not pursued, and even when valuable early work is undertaken it is frequently not followed up, hampering future development work. As the discussion on CD-ROMs shows, high production costs have led to a situation where commercial interests have driven development with unfortunate consequences for product quality (Warschauer 1996). Furthermore, considerable institutional barriers to technology implementation still exist in many educational contexts (Egbert, Paulus, and Nakamichi 2002; Garrett 2009). The discussion of videoconferencing draws attention to a further issue: Many educational institutions frequently lack the advanced network infrastructure, equipment, and support staff necessary for implementation of the latest technologies on a significant scale. Moreover, the successful implementation of new technologies requires the cooperation of teachers (Timuçin 2006). The issue of negative teacher attitudes toward the use of new computer technologies (Fernández Carballo-Calero 2001), and the need for teacher training (Moore, Morales, and Carel 1998), are further long-running issues that are frequently downplayed in the CALL literature. As this discussion has shown, teacher attitudes remain an important influence on the effective implementation of new innovations (Chambers and Bax 2006; Hlas and Vuksanovich 2007; Lam 2000). The lack of widespread teacher training in the use of CALL (Kessler 2007) perhaps explains the fact that the above issues remain constants in the literature. Finally, the relentless pace of technological change may constitute a barrier to the effective use of new technology in CALL (Levy 1997).

The Limited Influence of SLA Theory on CALL Research

The overview of the assimilation of new technologies conducted in this chapter draws attention to an important issue that requires acknowledgment in any assessment of new innovations in CALL, namely, the lack of any generally accepted theoretical framework to guide development work (Hubbard 2009, 5; Levy 2000, 170). However, this situation need not hamper research in CALL. As Gutierrez observes, systematic collaboration between researchers, and a theory-based approach to the application of new innovations in CALL remain essential if progress is to be made:

> Collaboration among second language teachers, software designers, and researchers, implies a cyclical process of constant research, design, implementation, and evaluation…this process should have its conceptual roots in sound second language acquisition theories and research, and should eventually also throw light upon these theories in order to gain a deeper understanding of language, its acquisition, and how language can be optimized in the classroom. (Gutierrez 2003, 94)

Huh and Hu identify important advantages of drawing on SLA theory as a means to inform research in CALL:

> It is important for CALL researchers to start with an SLA foundation and carry it through the study to the conclusion. Sound theoretical support helps researchers to generalize, validate, and apply their findings. (Huh and Hu 2005, 12)

Although the limited influence of SLA theory on the field of language education has been noted in the literature (Levy and Stockwell 2006), this phenomenon appears particularly acute in the case of CALL. Egbert (2005, 3) has identified this situation as hindering coherent development work:

> We have been thinking about ideas in this chapter and book over the last several years because we have looked into the computer-assisted language learning (CALL) research and have seen something is amiss. For example, although fine studies have been conducted on some topics, the research seems to be scattered across a wide area that a specific picture of what CALL is and does has not emerged. Also, the excitement, rigor, and applicability found in other areas of education research seem to be missing in CALL. Discussing why that might be, we discovered the lack of a coherent understanding of CALL; a tendency to do specific kinds

of research to the neglect of other questions, methods, and perspectives; and the logical but fallacious inclination to *test technologies rather than theories*. (Italics added)

The tendency in CALL research and pedagogy to focus on utilizing the latest technological innovations regardless of their appropriateness is a phenomenon that is noted in the literature (Levy 1997). Moreover, the tendency for technological advances to drive the bulk of development work in CALL continues, as Salaberry states:

> I believe that previous research on the efficacy of the use of technological tools for pedagogical purposes has been excessively focused on the technical capabilities of tools: technology-driven instruction. (Salaberry 2001, 51)

While experimentation has an important role to play in moving the field forward, the continuing tendency of many individual practitioners to take up the latest new technology while ignoring the valuable lessons that can be gleaned from past research has unfortunate consequences, as Levy observes:

> I believe the CALL community needs to build upon what has gone before, rather than be led purely by the capabilities of the latest technological innovation. With the almost monthly appearance of new hardware and software there can be a tendency for those interested in CALL materials development simply to pick up the latest machine or technological option and get to work on a project. If the technology has not been widely distributed, it is rather too easy to impress. Moreover, past work and valuable experience can be ignored or overlooked. It is usual, when commencing research in other fields, to review and extend the work of others, but with CALL the approach can sometimes be a little more cavalier. Over the last three decades, a substantial number of CALL programs have been created. The concepts and principles underpinning the best of these programs do not necessarily become obsolete when the computer that is used to run them is retired. In fact, the valuable knowledge and experience that has accumulated through this work needs to be absorbed and used to inform new projects in the future. (Levy 1997, xi)

The majority of the studies described in this chapter were to some degree theory-based. However, it is doubtful that this is the case in the field as a whole (Bax, 2003). Researchers have repeatedly emphasized that the influence of SLA theory on CALL development generally has been limited and that many studies lack a firm grounding in theories of language learning (Chapelle 1997; Doughty 1987; Felix 2005; Oxford 1995). This situation is reflected in the problematic nature of significant swathes of CALL research.

As was stated previously, the technology-driven nature of development work in CALL remains a cause for concern (Garrett 2009). Researchers draw attention to the tendency for projects to focus on the benefits of the latest new technology while disregarding potentially significant negative findings (Huh and Hu 2005). Such studies frequently fail to adequately explore the influence of contextual factors and other variables on learner behavior (Künzel 1995). The limitations of the research designs that are widely adopted in CALL research frequently make the findings of studies challenging to validate and generalize (Salaberry 2001). In order to avoid repeating the mistakes of the past, and to make progress in the future, there remains a need to more closely integrate theory and practice (Chapelle 2009; Colpaert 2010). In this context, any attempt to successfully implement technological innovations in CALL in the future should primarily be theory-led, rather than technology-led, and be based on a thorough appreciation of how CALL development has been conceptualized in the past. The following discussion examines conceptualizations of CALL proposed in the literature.

Conceptualizing the Use of New Technologies in CALL

In the CALL literature there have been relatively few attempts to recount the history of the field or conceptualize the role of new technological innovations in its development. Warschauer and Healey (1998) are among the few researchers to describe a history of CALL, the role of new technologies, and propose an agenda for the future. In their account of CALL development, Warschauer and Healy propose three phases. According to these researchers, the first phase, "behavioristic CALL," occurred in the 1960s and 1970s. This era was dominated by the use of mainframe computers and the prevailing influence of behaviorism. As was noted during the discussion of the PLATO system, computers in this period were used as a mechanical tutor that provided learners with access to drill-based practice and grammar tutorials. However, by the early 1980s, the influence of behaviorism fell into decline and this development coupled with the emergence of the PC gave rise to a new phase, "communicative CALL." Warschauer and Healey claim that during this phase development became influenced by new views of language learning that rejected behaviorism in favor of learner-centered discovery learning that focused on TL use, and the implicit teaching of grammar. This led to the emergence of new types of CALL software such as text reconstruction programs and simulations designed to operate on PCs. The final stage, "integrated CALL," arose in the 1980s as a reaction to the limitations of CALL use at the time where computers were perceived as making only a marginal impact. Another factor that stimulated this phase was the growing influence of what Warschauer and Healy describe as a socio-cognitive view of learning that privileges meaning-focused language use in authentic social contexts. The emergence in the 1990s of multimedia networked computers was seen as the central technological development in this final stage of CALL development, as it made possible the integration of the four skills more fully into the process of language learning.

The above account of CALL has proved valuable as means to conceptualize development in the field. However, it has been subject to criticism most notably by Bax (2003). This researcher has identified a number of problems including conceptual confusions, historical inconsistencies, and doubtful claims regarding the actual nature of CALL during each phase of development. In order to overcome these limitations Bax (2003, 21) has proposed an alternative analysis. In this account of CALL development, three distinct approaches are identified. The first is categorized as "restricted CALL." This covers a similar time period (the 1960s until the late 1970s) as that proposed by Warschauer and Healy in behaviorist CALL but incorporates a wider set of factors. Included are elements such as actual software and activity types (closed drills and quizzes) in use at the time, their position in the curriculum, teacher roles and attitudes, and the nature of feedback provided. The second approach, "open CALL," emerged in the early 1980s and continues to the present. This period is characterized by the continuation of elements of restricted CALL such as interaction with the computer, with the emergence of new elements including simulations and CMC tools. The final approach, "integrated CALL," is proposed as the goal of CALL development in the future. This entails what Bax describes as the emergence of a state of "normalization":

> This concept is relevant to any kind of technological innovation and refers to the stage when the technology becomes invisible, embedded in everyday practice and hence "normalized." (Bax 2003, 23)

Computer Games: Normalization in CALL?

Writing in 2003, Bax claimed that a state of widespread normalization had not yet been reached in CALL. More recent anecdotal evidence would appear to support this contention. Ioannou-Georgiou (2006, 383–384) reports that a summary of discussion in the IATEFL learning technology special interest group draws attention to the considerable barriers to the achievement of normalization. Factors identified include lack of access to appropriate hardware, software, and technical support. Other issues are the need for teacher training and the integration of technology as a central, as opposed to an optional, element in the syllabus. The persistence of these issues is emphasized elsewhere in the literature (Maftoon and Shahini 2012). Although the above factors remain barriers to the achievement of normalization in many educational settings, in recent years, there have been significant developments in computer technologies and SLA research that have created a new environment for CALL development. The expansion in Internet use and the emergence of low-cost computing devices such as tablet computers, and powerful mobile communication devices has greatly enhanced the accessibility of new computer technology. These phenomena have been accompanied by increasingly influential advances in education and SLA research that stress the central role played by language use and social interaction in language learning (Firth and Wagner 2007). Accompanying these developments is the dramatic expansion in the use of the Web 2.0 technologies that utilize the above tools. Of the Web 2.0 technologies now in widespread use, network-based multiplayer games are attracting increasing attention in educational research as they make possible new dynamic forms of social interaction. The emergence of large-scale computer gaming is perceived as a major development of great relevance to education and also to the field of CALL (Sykes, Oskoz, and Thorne 2008). The ubiquitous nature of network-based computer gaming, with its vast and diverse player base numbering in the millions coupled with its accessibility and widespread appeal would appear to make it a technology with the potential to achieve normalization.

The discussion in this chapter shows that any attempt to successfully implement new technological innovations in CALL in the future should draw on the lessons of the past. Moving forward, researchers investigating the use of computer games should be aware of the dangers inherent in technocentric thinking, recognize the challenging and complex nature of technology implementation, and acknowledge the limitations of past research. In evaluating the potential of new innovations in CALL there is a need to break with the approaches to development that have prevailed in the past. As this discussion has emphasized, a theory-led approach offers the prospect of rigorous principled development. In order to obtain a fuller and balanced appreciation of the potential of computer games in CALL there is a need to investigate the nature of computer gaming. The following chapter will first explore conceptions of play and games discussed in the literature. Theories that have been proposed to conceptualize computer gaming are then examined. Game genres that have been used in CALL are discussed as part of a wider attempt to establish if computer games represent a technology with the potential to achieve normalization.

CHAPTER 2

Computer Games: Definitions, Theories, Elements, and Genres

Computer Gaming: Toward a Definition

Early work on the nature of play and games was limited and restricted mainly to the fields of history and anthropology. It was not until the twentieth century that play and games began to be the object of systematic study. Pioneering work in conceptualizing play carried out by Huizinga (1955) emphasizes the central role of this activity in shaping human behavior, culture, and development. Huizinga defined play as:

> an activity which proceeds within certain limits of time and space, in visible order, according to rules freely accepted, and outside the sphere of necessity or material utility. The play-mood is one of rapture and enthusiasm, and is sacred or festive in accordance with the occasion. A feeling of exaltation and tension accompanies the action. (Huizinga 1955, 132)

This definition identifies the essential characteristics of play, namely, its voluntary nature, the sense that it occurs outside the everyday, and the absorption, satisfaction, and enjoyment engendered. Huizinga's ideas on the nature of play were taken up by Caillois (1961), who categorizes play into four forms: *agon* (competitive play such as sports), *alea* (chance-based play), mimicry (role-playing and make believe such as theater), and *ilinx* (play involving the physical, vertigo). In order to better comprehend play and games Caillois proposes a distinction between the essentially free nature of play and the rule-governed nature of games. Caillois draws attention to the variation in the complexity of games rules and distinguishes between games with simple rules (*paidia*) and games with more complex and structured rule systems (*ludus*).

More recent attempts to define play and games have stressed the interrelationships between the above concepts. In an example of this approach, Prensky (2002) argues that play is an engaging activity that is freely entered into. For Prensky participation in play provides pleasure and is also fun. From this perspective, games are conceived as a subset of both play and fun (Prensky 2001). Researchers further observe that games are complex phenomena that can be understood in a variety of ways (Whitton 2010; Zagal 2010). In attempting to define play and games researchers have emphasized differing aspects. For example, Salen and Zimmerman (2004, 80) view games as systems, while Sutton-Smith (2001) draws attention to the outcomes produced. In a somewhat different approach Koster (2005) argues that games should be perceived as puzzles. Although a consensus has yet to emerge, games are now frequently conceptualized as a form of play that is goal directed (Juul 2005). In this view, games provide enjoyment and pleasure through involvement in some form of competition. In this context Dempsey et al. (1996, 3) define a game as:

> a set of activities involving one or more players. It has goals, constraints, payoffs and consequences. A game is rule-guided and artificial in some respects. Finally, a game involves some aspect of competition, even if the competition is with oneself.

As has been pointed out in the literature, the definitions of play and games examined here while helpful, raise a number of issues. As Juul (2005, 10) observes, a problem with the categories of play proposed by Caillios is that almost all games involve a degree of competition and chance. Moreover, as Ang notes (2006, 307), the categories proposed by Caillios lack an explicit definition that accounts for the differences in complexity level among games rules. Although the concepts of play and games remain challenging to define (Zagal 2010), as the following discussion will show, the development of computer games has stimulated new research on the nature and qualities of play and games.

Although computer-based games first emerged in the early 1960's (Wolf and Perron 2003), it was the development of video games in the 1980's that led to increasing interest in the study of play in computer-based environments (Bryce and Rutter 2006). The forms of play made possible by computer games have led researchers to propose various definitions. For example, Frasca defines computer games as:

> any forms of computer-based entertainment software, either textual or image-based, using any electronic platform such as personal computers or consoles and involving one or multiple players in a physical or networked environment. (Frasca 2001, 4)

This definition while useful, does not sufficiently capture the variety of aspects that constitute play in a computer game. According to Fabricatore (2000, 3), the defining features of computer games are their interactive nature, and the fact that players must always engage in some form of opposition. A more comprehensive definition is provided by Juul (2005, 6–7), who claims that any game must incorporate at least some of the following features:

1. A rule-based formal system;
2. With variable and quantifiable outcomes;
3. Where different outcomes are assigned different values;
4. Where the players exert effort in order to influence the outcome;
5. The player feels emotionally attached to the outcome;
6. And the consequences of the activity are optional and negotiable.

As Juul notes (2005, 7), one advantage of the above model lies in its flexibility in defining what is or is not a game. Moreover, a further positive aspect of this definition is that it is transmedial in nature, and can therefore be applied to any media that are used for playing games, including computers. Although the above definition remains influential (Zagal 2010), as the following discussion will show, it is not accepted by all researchers. The variety of definitions examined here draws attention to the fact that to date, there is no generally agreed definition of computer gaming (Newman 2004). This situation is further reflected in the differing theoretical approaches to conceptualizing computer gaming proposed in the literature.

Computer Game Theories: Narratology and Ludology

Proponents of an influential conceptualization of computer games claim that, as many games can be viewed in a broad sense as stories, they should be investigated using theories of narrative (Atkins 2003; Laurel 1991; Murray 1997). This conception of computer gaming, known as narratology, takes the view that many games should be comprehended as novel forms of narrative. Narratologists approach the study of computer gaming from a variety of fields and theoretical perspectives. For example, Laurel (1991) applies the theories of theatre criticism to computers and argues for understanding computers as a medium. Laurel perceives computer games as a form of interactive drama and claims that they enable their users to play roles both as a performer and audience member. In a similar vein, Murray (1997), from the perspective of literary studies, claims that the computer represents a new medium for storytelling and argues for an expanded conception of storytelling she terms cyberdrama. An alternative approach is proposed by Jenkins (2003), who conceptualizes computer games as part of an ecology of transmedia storytelling that includes movies, comic books, and novels. Ryan (2002, 2006) also perceives narrative as a universal structure that transcends media. For Ryan computer games can be considered a form of narrative as they:

> present all the basic ingredients of narrative: characters, events, settings and trajectories leading from a beginning state to an end state. (Ryan 2006, 181)

Ryan (2002) proposes that narrative is based on mental images that are activated by signs. From this perspective, in a computer game these signs include the simulated world presented by the game and the user controlled avatars (characters) that interact and follow the story line (plot) of the game. Ryan claims that during play the actions of characters can initiate changes on a global scale in the game world narrative.

An alternative conception to the view of computer games as stories is proposed in the literature. This perspective, known as ludology, emphasizes that the study of computer games should constitute an independent academic field separate from other disciplines and that computer games are to be understood in their own terms (Simons 2007). For many ludologists, computer games should not be seen as narratives as Eskelinen observes:

> The basic components and aspects of the gaming situation, (are) essentially different from the basic constituents of narratives and dramatic situations. (Eskelinen 2001, 175)

Ludologists such as Eskelinen (2001) claim that conceptualizations of computer games must focus not on narratives, but on the players, and the rules and goals that define their behavior during the active process of gameplay. Some ludologists (Aarseth 2001), propose that computer games are fundamentally different to other types of game, and argue for the need to develop new conceptualizations of computer gaming that focus on understanding the nature of player activity. In an example of this approach, Frasca (1999, 2001) notes that while some games can produce stories, they are not the same as narratives. In attempts to define computer games from a ludic perspective, this researcher adapts the terminology proposed by Caillois. Frasca (2003) accepts that both play and games have rules but distinguishes between *ludus* games whose results are defined by winning and losing and *paidea* games where these results are not produced. Using these definitions, well-known examples of *ludus* computer game would include *Pac-Man* and *Mario Bros* while a *paidea* game would be *Simcity*.

Ludologists are also interested in exploring the interrelationship between game rules and play. Juul (2005, 5) argues that the major motivation for playing games is to overcome challenges. Juul claims that although game rules take different forms depending on the game, they provide these challenges through two types of game structure. The first type, emergent gameplay, is the most basic and occurs when a small number of simple rules combine to form a more complex and challenging series of variations. As Ang and Zaphiris (2006) note, chess is an example of a game of immergence where *paidea* and *ludus* rules combine. The second type, progression, is more recent, and occurs when the player must complete a sequence of separate challenges specified by the game designer in order to complete the game. A well-known example of a game based on a progression of *ludus* rules is the adventure game *Myst*.

In recent years, there have been attempts to unite narratology and ludology in an emergent theory of game studies (Simons 2007). Many ludologists, while holding to the view that not all computer games involve stories (Bizzocchi 2007), have largely come to accept that some types of computer games can produce narrative sequences, and that narratology may be a useful tool in understanding aspects of computer games (Ang 2006). In an example of this view, Juul (2005) argues for a new perspective on the relationship between narrative and player experience during gameplay. In this context, Juul (2005, 130–132) defines a four level hierarchy of representation in game worlds; abstract games such as *Tetris*, iconic games such as playing cards, incoherent games where the story is incomplete or contradictory such as *Donkey Kong*, and coherent where the story world is comprehensive and complete as in the contemporary online role-playing game *World of Warcraft*. For Juul the advantage of this approach is that it provides a conceptual framework to better comprehend the role of narrative in game design and player experience.

Computer Games: Fundamental Elements

Although researchers continue to debate the nature of play in computer games there is more general agreement on their distinguishing features. As Wolf and Perron (2003, 14–15) have noted, computer games incorporate a number of fundamental elements. As table 2.1 shows, these combine to provide the environment presented by a computer game. The first of these elements is the graphics. This term is used to describe the dynamic visual display presented to a game player. The second element, the interface,

Table 2.1 Fundamental elements of computer games

Graphics	Visual display presented to a player
Interface	Hardware and on-screen elements required for gameplay
Player activity	Physical and mental activity produced by gameplay
Algorithm	The software program that controls the graphics, sound, and play activity

describes any hardware or on-screen graphical elements such as menus and buttons that a player must use in order to play the game. The interface facilitates the third element, player activity. This term describes the physical and mental activity elicited by playing a game. Player activity is shaped by the fourth element, the algorithm. This describes the software program that controls the graphics and sound. The algorithm further influences player behavior.

Of the elements proposed by Wolf and Perron (2003), player activity is of great interest to researchers due to its association with learning. Recent research has attempted to establish the key attributes of computer games that are claimed to play a role in facilitating learning. These factors will be examined at a later stage of this discussion. The potential of certain types of computer games to facilitate learning has been investigated by researchers working in a variety of disciplines. Researchers in the field of CALL have also explored the use of various types of computer games.

Computer Game Genres Utilized in CALL

The literature on game genres reveals that there are many types of computer games, each with their own distinct qualities (Griffith 1996). A wide variety of game categories and subcategories have been proposed. However, a consensus has yet to emerge regarding generally accepted game classifications (Berens and Howard 2001). The discussion will now focus on a description of the major types of computer games that have been subject to investigation in CALL research. The games examined contain features identified in the literature as significant. These include the operation of rules, overcoming obstacles, some element of competition, and intrinsic motivation. An overview and analysis of significant findings from learner-based studies on the use of the games described in the following discussion will be provided in chapters 5 and 6.

Text Manipulation

Text-manipulation games were among the first computer games to be explored in CALL research (Johns and Wang 1999). An early paper by Morrison (1984) describes the interactive text-manipulation game *Gapper*. As table 2.2 shows, this game is designed for use on a microcomputer. The game is based on a cloze procedure and utilizes a points system where the player gains points by correctly typing in words missing from a text inputted by the teacher. In the first stage of the game, players are presented with comprehension questions relating to the meaning of a passage. Players then move on to a timed reading. The longer the player takes the more points are deducted from their score. At this stage, if a player takes too long to read the text they can lose the game. In the following comprehension check stage, players must complete five multiple-choice questions relating to the content of the previously encountered comprehension questions. On conclusion of this activity, the original passage is then displayed with some words missing. Learners gain points for correctly filling in the missing words. They can also lose points for incorrect answers. If the player completes all the missing words correctly they can move on to the final stage of the game, where all the words from the original passage are deleted.

CALL researchers have investigated the use of various text-manipulation games in learner-based research. In an example of this approach Piper (1986) investigated learner use of three games. The gap-filling game *Clozemaster* presents the player with a text of up to 50 lines where words are removed at regular intervals. In order to complete the game, the

Table 2.2 Text-manipulation games utilized in CALL

Game type	Study	Title	Language	Platform
Text manipulation	Morrison (1984)	*Gapper*	English	Microcomputer
	Piper (1986)	*Clozemaster Copywrite Vocabulary*	English	BBC B Microcomputer
	Legenhausen and Wolff (1990)	*Storyboard*	English	PC
	Higgins, Lawrie, and White (1999)	*Sequitur*	English	PC
	Johns and Wang (1999)	*Bilingual Sentence Shuffler*	English	PC

player must type in the missing words. The length of missing words is not revealed, and at least one attempt to input each missing word is required. At any stage during the game, the player can request hints in the form of individual letters or whole words. *Copywrite* presents the player with a format that is similar to *Clozemaster*. However, it incorporates a basic scoring procedure. Piper also examined learner use of the game *Vocabulary* where learners are required to reorder sentences containing vocabulary focusing on banking.

Legenhausen and Wolff (1990) used a version of the game *Storyboard* (Higgins and Johns 1984) with EFL students. In *Storyboard* the player is presented with a text that is displayed in the form of dashes and punctuation. The player is supplied with a prompt inviting them to guess a word. If the player inputs a word that appears in the text all instances of that word are then displayed. The game contains a help option where players can request display of the first missing word and all occurrences of specified prefixes or suffixes. Players can also request that the complete text be displayed on-screen for a period of ten seconds.

Higgins, Lawrie, and White (1999) examined use of the reordering software game *Sequitur*. In this text-manipulation game learners log on using their real names or a nickname. After completing the entry protocol the player is provided with a line of text from a story that is correct up to a certain point. In order to progress, the player must choose the most suitable continuation from three possible choices. If a correct selection is made, the selected text is added and more continuations are offered. If an incorrect selection is made the player must chose an alternative. The game provides a record keeping function that displays, at the end of each session, correct and incorrect selections.

Research conducted by Johns and Wang (1999) describes use of the text-manipulation program *Bilingual Sentence Shuffler*. In this game, players encounter an authentic English text of between three to a maximum of eight sentences where the sentences have been mixed up. The goal of the game is for the player to correctly reorder the sentences using the drag-and-drop feature. This game contains a number of innovate features. A gambling scoring system is utilized that invites the player to predict the correct order of all the sentences. Players have access to a scratchpad facility that enables experimentation with different orderings. Parallel translation of the English text selected is provided in Chinese. Individual players can select texts of varying levels of difficulty using the on-screen menu. The game further provides a logging feature that facilitates the collection of player performance data.

Text-Based Adventure

As can be observed in table 2.3, CALL researchers have investigated a number of text-based adventure games. G. Jones (1986) describes the experimental use of the adventure game *Yellow River Kingdom* with EFL learners. In this game, an on-screen virtual world is described in text. The game also incorporates limited graphics. Players adopt the role of the ruler of a hypothetical kingdom that is prone to flooding and attacks from thieves. The player must make decisions regarding the allocation of limited resources. For example, the ruler has to decide the proportions of the population that engage in the tasks of rice planting, defense, and maintaining the dykes. Once decisions have been inputted the game reports the consequences on-screen. These can include, for example, a good rice season or attacks from bandits. The goal of the game is to maintain the population at a high level for as long as possible. If the player fails to maintain the population disasters can ensue.

Culley, Mulford, and Milbury-Steen (1986) explored use of a French version of the commercial text adventure game *Mystery House*. This game provides access to a theme and text-based world. On entering the game, a player is presented with a textual description of a virtual world. They are then required to take a course of action by typing a sentence. If the action is possible the game world is altered in some way and the player is then provided with the option of undertaking different courses of action. The selection of

Table 2.3   Text-based adventure games utilized in CALL

Game type	Study	Title	Language	Platform
Text-based adventure	G. Jones (1986)	*Yellow River Kingdom*	English	BBC microcomputer
	Culley, Mulford, and Milbury-Steen (1986)	*Mystery House*	French	PC, mainframe
	Palmberg (1988)	*Pirate Cove*	English	PC
	Molla, A. Sanders, and R. Sanders (1988)	*Spion*	German	IBM PC
	Cheung and Harrison (1992)	*Colossal Adventure*	English	PC
	Neville, Shelton, and McInnis (2009)	*Ausflug Nach Munchen*	German	PC, Laptop

a particular option influences the game world in different ways and leads to further options. If the request is not possible the player is provided with an explanation. The game provides access to a number of different locations. To achieve game goals, players are required to traverse virtual space in order to obtain and manipulate virtual objects that assist their advancement in the game. These objects can be obtained through buying and selling.

Palmberg (1988) investigated use of the text-based adventure game *Pirate Cove*. This game utilizes a pirate theme and the vocabulary required to play the game consists of 118 English words. During gameplay, players utilize keyboard commands to navigate around ten islands displayed on an on-screen map with the ultimate goal of locating a hidden treasure chest. The locations of the islands change with each game. As players explore virtual space they are presented with a number of differing options on how to proceed. On selecting an option, players are required to undertake various tasks such as, for example, searching swamps, village huts, or sunken ships. They can manipulate virtual objects and use them to solve puzzles. In this game players must further deal with unexpected difficulties such as encountering a severe storm or a sea monster.

Molla, A. Sanders, and R. Sanders (1988) describe a pilot project on the use of the prototype text-based adventure game *Spion*. This interactive fiction game is designed to facilitate the study of German by intermediate- and advanced-level students. *Spion* is based on a spy theme and utilizes simple graphics. On entering, players are provided with an introductory tutorial in German that describes game instructions and protocols. In order to win the game, learners undertake the following activities. They must navigate through a simulation of Berlin using specific keyboard commands, make decisions appropriate to the scenarios presented, and direct a fictitious secret agent. In responding to the agent's questions, players must use correct German sentences or the desired action is not accomplished. This game utilizes artificial intelligence (AI) techniques in order to parse student responses.

Cheung and Harrison (1992) examined use of the text-based adventure game *Colossal Adventure*. This interactive fiction game provides players with access to a virtual world based on an imaginary cave. On entering, a player adopts the role of a game character. In order to play, a player enters simple keyboard commands and reacts to the responses generated by the game. As they advance through the game, players encounter fantasy characters described in text such as elves, trolls, and dwarves that populate the cave. Players can navigate around the cave, engage in combat, solve puzzles, and utilize magic with the ultimate goal of locating a number of treasures.

Neville, Shelton, and McInnis (2009) explored use of the game *Ausflug Nach München* that is designed for learners of German as a foreign language.

In contrast to the fantasy theme presented by some other text-based adventure games, this game provides immersion in a realistic scenario where an exchange student living in Germany must undertake a sightseeing trip to Munich. During gameplay the player must navigate around the environment and successfully undertake a number of authentic tasks. These include parking a bicycle, buying the correct train ticket, finding a book to read, and locating the correct train platform. Players must also interact with game generated characters from minority cultures as they progress through the game.

Simulation

As table 2.4 shows, simulation games have been used in CALL research. Li and Topolewski (2002) describe a simulation game for the teaching of English as foreign language to children. These researchers report on the features of *Zip & Terry*, a game that incorporates a strong narrative element with a graphically rich 2D simulated world populated by various animated characters designed to appeal to children. The game further utilizes speech recognition technology. In *Zip & Terry* an alien from another planet (Zip) is stranded on earth after their spaceship crashes into the Broccoli family home. The goal of the game is for Zip to collect a number of spare parts for his spaceship. These appear when a task is completed successfully. The collection of spare parts enables Zip to eventually repair his spaceship in order to return home. On entering the game, a player assumes the role of Zip who is required to undertake a series of language tasks. For example, the player can engage in conversations with members of the Broccoli family using phrases selected from a phrase book. They

Table 2.4   Simulation games utilized in CALL

Game type	Study	Title	Language	Platform
2D and 3D simulation	Li and Topolewski (2002)	*Zip & Terry*	English	PC
	Miller and Hegelheimer (2006)	*The Sims*	English	PC, Laptop or Console
	Ranalli (2008)		English	PC, Laptop or Console
	Anderson et al. (2008)	*America's Army*	English	PC, Laptop
	Coleman (2002)	*SimCopter*	English	PC, Laptop

can give verbal commands to a virtual pet that responds in real time if the command is appropriate. Other game activities include playing card games designed to facilitate the memorization of nouns and pronouns, the study of verbs by surfing television channels, taking part in a quiz, and taking a job as salesman.

Computer games that present simulations of real-life environments and situations have also been a focus of CALL research. Studies undertaken by Miller and Hegelheimer (2006), and Ranalli (2008), explored the use of the well-known social simulation game *The Sims*. In this open-ended game a player must guide the life of a virtual person or persons as they encounter life's challenges. Individual players are supplied with customizable personal avatars known in the game as Sims. These can move through virtual space, manipulate virtual objects, and interact with other players. Sims must make decisions to prolong their life in the game. For example, they must find jobs, eat, shop, exercise, and resolve interpersonal issues. Sims can also undertake various activities such as decorating their virtual homes with furniture and appliances. *The Sims* provides players with access to a graphically rich simulation of a suburban setting that uses a combination of 2D and 3D graphics. Although originally developed for use on desktop computers, more recent versions have been ported for use on consoles.

Anderson et al. (2008) made use of the in-game tutorials and training mission element of the freeware simulation game *America's Army*. On entering the game, players undertake a number of in-game tutorials that provide exposure to authentic dialog. The initial tutorial is provided by a 3D avatar instructor and focuses on how to play the game effectively. Additional tutorials are also provided by a virtual instructor and deal with aspects of basic military training such as marksmanship, and first aid. On completion of the initial tutorials, players move on to undertake realistic simulated training missions that require players to follow orders quickly and accurately in order to progress in the game.

Another type of simulation game that has been utilized in CALL is the single player flight simulator game *SimCopter*. In a study reported by Coleman (2002) a demo version of this game was used as a means to promote the writing skills of language learners. In *SimCopter* a player assumes the role of a pilot who must fly their helicopter around a 3D virtual city. The gameplay revolves around dealing with various software-generated tasks including rescues, traffic jams, fires, catching criminals, and medical emergencies. Successful completion of these tasks enables a player to accumulate money and points. These allow players to purchase better equipment and move to higher levels in the game that offer more challenging activities.

First-Person Shooter

As can be observed in table 2.5, a further type of computer game that has been examined in experimental CALL research is the First-Person Shooter. In this genre, the player takes part in combat against an attacker in a simulated 2D or 3D desktop world using some kind of weapon from a first person perspective. A subgenre of this type of game *House of the Dead* involves shooting attacking zombies to gain points. This game has been adapted for use in the teaching of Japanese (Stubbs 2003). A modified educational version of the original *House of the Dead* game *The Typing of the Dead* was used where weapon-based combat is replaced by typing out words or phrases in order to kill attacking zombies. In *Kana no Senshi* players are presented with a modified version of *The Typing of the Dead* interface. During the game they must type out English translations of the on-screen hiragana and katakana characters associated with each zombie in order to avoid being killed.

3D Adventure

As table 2.5 shows, single player adventure games that utilize high quality 3D graphics, avatars, and audio have also been used in CALL. In an example of this approach, Chen and Yang (2011), examined learner play in the 3D adventure game *Bone*. In this game, players are immersed in an interactive story that revolves around the adventures of three animated characters who, after being chased out their hometown, embark on a journey through a graphically rich 3D virtual world. On their travels the characters become separated and the narrative describes their attempts to find each other. In the game, players encounter various puzzles that must be solved in order for the characters to progress in the game. They must also find ways to escape from mysterious enemies who attack them.

Massively Multiplayer Online Role-Playing Games (MMORPGs)

The design of MMORPGs draws on early computer-based multiplayer adventure games known as multi-user dungeons (henceforth MUDs). MUDs provide access to persistent 2D virtual game worlds based on a fantasy theme (Bartle 2003). In a MUD a player can view text-based descriptions of locations, objects, and other players. The player adopts a customizable online character that presents a unique persona to other players. This character can engage in role-play and real-time communication with other players and non-player agents through the use of text chat.

Table 2.5 2D and 3D computer games utilized in CALL

Game type	Study	Title	Language	Platform
First-person shooter	Stubbs (2003)	Kana No Senshi	Japanese	PC, Laptop
3D adventure	Chen and Yang (2011)	Bone	English	PC, Laptop
Role-play including massively multiplayer online role-playing games (MMORPGs)	Rankin, Gold, and Gooch (2006)	Ever Quest II	English	PC, Laptop, Mobile device, Console
	Thorne (2008)	World of Warcraft	English	PC, Laptop, Mobile device, Console
	Piirainen-Marsh and Tainio (2009)	Final Fantasy X	English	Console, PC, Mobile device
	Suh, S. Kim, and N. Kim (2010)	Nori School	English	PC
	Reinders and Wattana (2011)	Ragnarok Online	English	PC, Laptop
Multiuser virtual environments (MUVEs)	Johnson (2007)	Tactical Iraqi	Arabic	PC, Laptop
	Zheng et al. (2009)	Quest Atlantis	English	PC, Laptop
	Liang (2011)	Erie Isle	English	PC, Laptop
Sports	deHaan (2005)	Jiikyoo Powafuru Pro Yakkyu 6	Japanese	Console
Rhythm	deHaan, Reed, and Kuwada (2010)	Parappa the Rapper 2	English	Console

MUD characters can navigate virtual space, manipulate virtual objects, and undertake purposeful interaction through the use of specific typed commands. In a MUD, the goal of the player is to advance to higher levels in the game hierarchy through the successful completion of tasks known as quests. Quests involve a wide variety of tasks such as solving puzzles, engaging in combat with other players, and trading virtual commodities. These activities frequently require collaboration with other players and take place under the auspices of game-based social organizations known as guilds. Guild membership is necessary in order to successfully undertake the increasingly complex quests that are encountered as players advance in the game. The MUD concept was developed further with the introduction of object-orientated MUDs known as MOOs (Hayes and Holmevik 2001). In a MOO, a player can create additional content within a MUD game world (Peterson 2001).

MMORPGs incorporate many of the features of MUDs and MOOs. For example, in popular MMORPGs, such as *World of Warcraft*, the fantasy theme adopted in many MUDs is retained. Players can use unique online characters that engage in role-play and real-time communication with other players and non-player agents. Moreover, players can undertake a wide range of quests and have opportunities to participate in guilds. As is the case in MUDs, guild membership facilitates progression in the game hierarchy. Contemporary MMORPGs now take advantage of a number of advances in computer technologies. Although text chat is retained, players of many MMORPGs now have access to audio chat. Furthermore, the majority of MMORPGs now provide access to 3D graphical user interfaces of very high quality (Peterson 2010). Customizable 3D avatars that enhance the sense of immersion and emotional involvement experienced by players have replaced text-based characters. MMORPGs are designed to accommodate the large numbers of players made possible by the expansion of the Internet and the emergence of mobile communication devices such as smart phones and tablet computers. At present, large numbers of players can be accommodated within most MMORPG worlds at any given time. As table 2.5 shows, MMORPGs have been explored in a number of learner-based CALL projects. Early exploratory research carried out by Rankin, Gold, and Gooch (2006) investigated learner play in *Ever Quest II*. Thorne (2008) reported on the game-related interaction of two players in *World of Warcraft*. Piirainen-Marsh and Tainio (2009) reported on the use of a console version of a role-playing game in the *Final Fantasy* series that incorporates many features found in MMORPGs. In more recent studies, Suh, S. Kim, and N. Kim (2010) examined play in *Nori School* and Reinders and Wattana (2011) explored the use of a modified version of *Runescape*.

Multi-User Virtual Environments (MUVEs)

MUVEs provide access to persistent high quality 3D simulations of virtual worlds that can contain large numbers of users (Cooke-Plagwitz 2008). As object-orientated environments, MUVEs incorporate user-created content. Most MUVEs are designed primarily as environments for real-time communication and provide both text and voice chat tools (Peterson 2011). Users can make use of personal avatars that facilitate role-play and immersion. These avatars can also undertake navigation and communication in real time. Although not specially designed as games, a number of MUVEs have been modified to provide access to games designed to facilitate language learning. In an example of this approach, shown in table 2.5, Zheng et al. (2009) examined learner questing in the modified MUVE *Quest Atlantis*. Johnson (2007) investigated learner use of the game elements of a MUVE-based training system *Tactical Iraqi*. Liang (2011) analyzed learner language play in *Erie Isle*, a role-play game created within the MUVE *Second Life*.

Sports

The console-based Japanese language sports game *Jiikyoo Powafuru Pro Yakkyu 6* (Announcing Powerful Pro Baseball 6) has been implemented in experimental CALL research (deHaan 2005). In this baseball game, players encounter a simulation of a baseball stadium that is populated by cartoon players based on Japanese anime designs. Three announcers appear in the game: an umpire who calls the pitches, a male commentator who provides a running commentary, and a female stadium announcer who introduces each batter and comments on their batting statistics. Players have the option of controlling a number of game features. For example, selecting the next hitter, allowing injuries, and setting the game's level of difficulty. The game has two player modes, batter and fielder. In batter mode, the player controls batting behaviors and running. In fielding mode, the player controls pitching and the position of both infield and outfield fielders. The interface displays game information such as scores and the number of runners in real time.

Rhythm

deHaan, Reed, and Kuwada (2010) conducted a study on the use of the console-based commercial rhythm game *Parappa the Rapper 2*. In this game, players are immersed in a 3D environment with a background story that contains aural and textual language in the form of a sequence of brief

English raps and accompanying subtitles. Game audio is triggered by a pressing a button on the console. During gameplay the player is required to keep up with a musical rhythm. The game is level based, with each level represented by a short rap that the player must complete at the correct time and in sequence by pressing the control button on their game console at the appropriate moment. If the player does not respond in time or fails to maintain the correct sequence they are unable to progress. The section of the game explored in the above study simulates a fast-food outlet that contains 2D avatars, a score meter, rhythm meter, and subtitles of game lyrics. The gameplay revolves around completing a sequence of brief rap-based instructions on how to make a fast-food meal. When the player presses a button on their console, audio of a word appropriate to the context is played, and this is accompanied by a real-time action made by an avatar in the simulation, for example, the chef avatar flips a burger. A button press made at an appropriate time when the word and action correspond produces an on-screen animation, a sound effect, and an increase in the player's total score.

This chapter has examined influential conceptualizations of play and games proposed in the literature and has emphasized that a generally accepted definition of computer gaming has yet to emerge. The differing definitions proposed to account for computer gaming examined in this discussion highlight the complex nature of the phenomenon. The discussion draws attention to the fundamental elements of computer games and has described the range of game genres that have been investigated in CALL research. The following chapter first identifies key features of computer games that claimed to play a role in learning. The discussion further explores theories proposed to justify the use of computer games as means to support learning. This is followed by an analysis of the significant findings of research studies that have focused on investigating the relationship between computer games and learning.

CHAPTER 3

Computer Games and Learning

Play, Games, and Learning

Educational research has long emphasized the connection between play, games, and learning. Piaget (1961) classified games into three types: games that involve physical exercise, symbolic games where the player uses their imagination, and games where the play is governed by the operation of rules. For Piaget, the particular form of play that occurs in rule-bound games is associated with the socialization that facilitates human learning. From this perspective, play is primarily associated with children and is first undertaken purely for pleasure. However, when the child begins to participate in more organized rule-governed forms of play that require adult-like socialization, cognitive development may be facilitated. The emergence and spread of video games in the 1980s led researchers to speculate that features of computer games could facilitate learning. In an example of this early work, the computer game studies theorist Crawford (1984) proposed that computer games encompass four key qualities: representation (meaning that games encompass a closed system that presents a subset of reality), interaction (the effects caused by gameplay), conflict, and safety. This researcher argued that these elements combine in a computer game to elicit a highly engaging form of play and that a major motivation of participation in computer gaming is to learn. This period further witnessed the initiation of research that examined from the perspective of cognitive science, the possible linkages between participation in computer gaming and human learning. In a well-received book, Greenfield (1984) investigated the effects of computer games on children. Greenfield claimed that children who played computer games regularly developed enhanced motor skills. Dorval and Pépin (1986) conducted research that suggests playing computer games supports spatial visualization. During this period, research was undertaken on the use of computer games in classroom contexts. Silvern (1986) claimed that playing computer games supports learning processes such as hypothesis formation and generalizing conclusions. Later theorists, who have also attempted to identify the characteristics of computer games that are claimed to support learning, took up this early work. An examination of this more recent research is conducted in the following discussion.

Computer Games and Human Learning

As was observed in the previous section, the rise of computer games in the 1980s led to claims that they have great potential as a means to facilitate learning. The dramatic expansion of computer gaming in recent years has stimulated the creation of an extensive and growing body of research conducted from a wide variety of perspectives that explores the educational potential of games. Game studies theorists have long argued that many types of computer games are valuable tools for learning. In the field of literacy studies, influential scholars argue that computer games provide for new forms of literacy conducive to learning (Squire and Jenkins 2003). Moreover, theorists working in the emerging field of digital media and learning such as Gee (2009a) have drawn on developments in cognitive science in order to propose a credible rationale for the use of certain types of computer games in education (Gee 2007b). This phenomenon has been accompanied by increasing claims that computer games can support a powerful and effective form of learning (Squire 2011). A number of game studies theorists are associated with this perspective; among these researchers the work of Prensky is noteworthy, and it is to an examination of relevant aspects of his work that this discussion will now turn.

Computer Games and Learning: The Game Studies Perspective

Researchers working in the field of game studies have drawn attention to the potential of computers games as educational tools. As was noted previously, Crawford (1984) argued that some types of computer games incorporate elements that support learning. More recently, Juul (2005, 5) has argued that playing a computer game is a learning experience. Of the contemporary game studies theorists who have attempted to explore the linkages between computer gaming and learning the work of Prensky (2001, 2002, 2006a,

2006b) remains influential. For Prensky, play as an activity is intimately involved in learning at a fundamental level:

> Play has a deep biological, evolutionary important, function, which has to do specifically with learning. (Prensky 2001, 112)

In this view, the enjoyment and pleasure engendered by undertaking play not only elicits a high degree of involvement, it can also result in learning. Prensky (2002) emphasizes the interconnectedness of play and fun and the central role of these factors in human learning. As noted in chapter 2, Prensky conceives of games as a type of play, and claims that when a game is fun the enjoyment created has beneficial effects that can result in learning:

> So fun—in the sense of enjoyment and pleasure—puts us in a relaxed receptive state of mind for learning. Play, in addition to providing pleasure, increases our involvement, which also helps us learn. (Prensky 2001, 117)

Prensky (2006b) argues that the young people of today who have grown up in the era of the Internet and advanced computer technologies are "digital natives" who learn most effectively when using new computer and communication technologies. Prensky (2001) further asserts that of these new technologies, computer games in particular have a number of qualities that combine during gameplay to make them not only engaging but also effective tools for learning.

As can be observed in table 3.1, Prensky (2001, 118–124) identifies the following elements of games as having the potential, when combined, to facilitate learning. In common with a number of game studies theorists such as Salen and Zimmerman (2004) and Frasca (1999), Prensky argues that rules distinguish games from other kinds of unstructured play as they set limitations, and provide a framework that determines player behavior. In the context of computer gaming, rules are intrinsic to the game and require all players to follow certain paths. Rules are closely linked to another element of games that is involved in learning—goals. According to Prensky, goals are an integral part of games and their presence is contrasted with simulations that although they can be played, frequently have no explicit goals provided by their designers. Echoing claims made by early researchers who stress the close relationship between motivation and learning (Malone 1981), Prensky proposes that manifestations of goals in games such as, for example, scoring systems are, in part, responsible for the high degree of motivation that is frequently displayed by game players. Prensky identifies outcomes and feedback as further essential elements of games that contribute to learning.

Table 3.1 Prensky's structural elements of computer games involved in learning

Element	Hypothesized role in learning
Rules	Provide limits and a framework that guides player behavior
Goals and objectives	Provide motivation
Outcomes and feedback	Elicit emotional investment
Conflict/Competition/ Challenge/Opposition	Support problem solving and stimulate interest and involvement
Interaction	Supports the formation of game-based social groups
Representation or story	Enhance engagement

Outcomes provide a measure of progress toward game goals, and establish if a player has won or lost. They also influence the emotions associated with victory or loss and are therefore claimed to enhance the appeal of games. Moreover, in Prensky's view, feedback is closely related to learning in computer games. Feedback can take a variety of forms including scores, graphics, or audio effects. When a change in the game world occurs through a player action, the feedback generated provides the mechanism by which players learn about the game. For Prensky, feedback enables players to understand if they are winning or losing, and this supports learning as players continually strive to improve their level and mastery of the game.

The conflict and opposition provided by many games are additional elements of game structure that stimulate and maintain engagement. These are linked to the challenge and opposition provided. Taken as a whole, Prensky claims these factors at a fundamental level involve problem solving and assume an important role in maintaining player interest and excitement during gameplay. Prensky further emphasizes the interactive nature of games. Interactivity is conceived as both the feedback provided by games and their inherently social nature. For Prensky, the rise of multiplayer games and associated online player communities demonstrates that many games promote the creation of social groups that provide members with opportunities for learning. The final element of games identified by Prensky is described as representation. In essence, this term is used to describe the narrative and fantasy elements found in many types of computer games. Prensky argues that in well-designed computer games the above elements combine to produce the intense engagement and pleasure that is characteristic of learning in the flow states described by Csikszentmihalyi (1990).

Computer Games and Learning: The Digital Media Perspective

The rise of new forms of digital media and their influence on education and society at large has attracted increasing attention from researchers. Among scholars who have investigated the relationship between forms of new digital media and learning, the work of Gee (2007b) remains particularly influential. The work of this theorist is wide ranging and includes exploration of the nature of human cognition (Gee 1992), literacy (Gee 1996), and discourse (Gee 1999). The discussion in this section first provides an overview of common themes associated with Gee's conception of human learning. This will be followed by examination of his views on the relationship between learning and computer games. The final part of this section will examine Gee's views on the possibilities of using computer games as a means to promote language learning.

Gee does not accept the behaviorist view of cognition that perceives learning as exclusively an inner mental phenomenon that is largely the product of individual responses to external stimuli. Instead he emphasizes more recent accounts of human learning that have been developed in the fields of the learning sciences, new literacy studies, and situated cognition (Gee 2007b, 2009a, 2009b). Gee's work reflects a synthesis and extension of relevant work in these areas and draws on the findings of research conducted from the perspective of situated cognition, to argue that learning is based on embodied experience rather than the storage and retrieval of conceptual knowledge:

> Human understanding, then, is not primarily a matter of storing general concepts in the head or applying abstract rules to experience. Rather, humans think, understand, and learn best when they use their prior experiences (so they must have some) as a guide to prepare themselves for action. (Gee 2009a, 17)

Influenced by work conducted by researchers working in the field of the learning sciences, he further claims that learning is deeply embedded in the material, social, and cultural world (Gee 2007b). Gee views the activities of reading and writing as playing a central role in learning. However, in common with many new literacy theorists, he perceives these activities as not only mental phenomena but also as social and cultural practices. These practices are intimately bound up with the social activities of discourse communities and have significant economic, historical, and political implications.

Another important element of Gee's conception of learning is an emphasis on connectionism. For Gee, human beings are pattern recognizers and this activity plays an important role in learning:

> Humans—like connectionist computers—look for patterns in the elements of their experiences in the world and, as they have more and more experiences, find deeper and more subtle patterns, patterns that help predict what might happen in the future when they act to accomplish goals. (Gee 2009a, 18)

The above perspective and the approaches to cognition described here play a central role in Gee's conceptualization of learning with new digital media and with computer games in particular:

> I believe that these three areas capture central truths about the human mind and human learning and that these truths are well represented in the ways in which good video games are learned and played. (Gee 2007b, 9)

In an extensive body of research, Gee has explored the use of computer games as educational tools. Gee (2005, 2007b) draws attention to the challenge provided by many genres of computer games and notes the high degree of motivation engendered. Gee hypothesizes that certain types of good computer games incorporate a number of learning principles that facilitate what he describes as "deep learning." This is a form of learning that occurs when:

> game play elements that initially seem simple, and easy to learn, become more complex the more the player comes to master them. (Gee 2007a, 6)

Moreover, he further claims that video games based on the above principles are not only a form of entertainment; they also have the potential to evolve into effective learning environments for the twenty-first century in both in-school and out-of-school contexts (2007b).

Gee (2005, 2007b) identifies a number of general principles inherent in effective learning that are realized in well-designed computer games. As table 3.2 shows, these are grouped under three categories. The first of these, "empowered learners," includes the principles of "co-design," "customize," "identity," and "manipulation and distributed knowledge." The principle of co-design refers to learning environments where the learner plays an active rather than passive role. Computer games provide semiotic domains that are interactive and learner-centered in nature. This supports critical learning as learners feel they are actively cocreating the game world they are

Table 3.2 Gee's learning principles realized in computer games

Category	Empowered Learners	Problem Solving	Understanding
Principles	Co-design	Well-ordered problems	System thinking
	Customize	Pleasantly frustrating	Meaning as action image
	Identity	Cycles of expertise	
	Manipulation and distributed knowledge	Information on demand and just in time	
		Fish tanks	
		Sandboxes	
		Skills as strategies	

experiencing. The customize principle states that the most effective learning occurs when learners are provided with opportunities to try new styles of learning and decide by themselves how their learning will proceed. This principle is embedded in many computer games where the game supports different learning styles and adaption. The identity principle describes the deep learning produced when learners adopt a new identity that they value. Many computer games offer players the chance to assume and develop new online identities through the provision of individual game characters. This aspect of play in computer games is reflected in the high degree of engagement and commitment that is a well-documented feature of player behavior. Manipulation and distributed knowledge describe the sense of empowerment engendered by the use of tools at a distance. These principles operate in games that provide players with enhanced opportunities to manipulate personal avatars and virtual objects that serve as smart tools that can be used to fulfill player goals. Many types of computer games involve virtual action at a distance and incorporate smart tools that act as knowledge repositories. These factors facilitate learning by enhancing immersion in the game world, and also provide access to knowledge that is distributed among other players and in virtual tools. Well-designed computer games create contexts where this knowledge must be shared and integrated in order to achieve successful outcomes.

The second category proposed by Gee, "problem solving," contains the principles of "well-ordered problems," "pleasantly frustrating," "cycles of expertise," "information on demand and just in time," "fish tanks," "sandboxes," and "skills as strategies." The first of these, well-ordered problems, is based on the principle that learning is most effective when learners encounter problems in a structured way, so that they are guided into developing hypotheses that are useful in dealing with more challenging problems in the future. Many computer games provide this type of environment as early problems are designed in a manner that encourages the development of good generalizations that are useful in dealing with the more demanding challenges encountered in later stages of the game. The principle pleasantly frustrating describes the view that learning is facilitated when learners encounter problems that are challenging but achievable. Computer games frequently present problems of this sort. They also supply feedback on player performance, supporting motivation and continued participation. The cycles of expertise principle refers to the concept that expertise is the product of repeated cycles of practicing skills, mastering them, and then encountering new challenges that require the development of new skills. When skills become nearly automatic and then fail when encountering a new problem, the learner is challenged to repeat the process by integrating both old and new skills, repeating the cycle. Computer games are frequently designed to support these cycles by providing extensive practice, followed by tests of mastery. On reaching a higher level in a game, players confront new challenges that require further practice. This process is seen as building expertise. Information on demand and just in time refers to the principle that verbal and written information supports learning best when it is provided in a context where it is required and can be put to immediate use. Computer games provide essential information in this way. In many computer games, players learn about the game by first experiencing playing it and by consulting in-game resources.

The fish tanks principle refers to the idea that the complex systems operating in the real world are best comprehended by first providing simplified systems that focus on central variables and relationships. Computer games offer novice players fish tanks in the form of in-game tutorials. These enable players to understand the key elements and features of the game without being overwhelmed by them. Sandboxes are the safe areas in games where learners can experiment, but where the risks and pressures associated with learning in the real world are greatly reduced. Computer games provide novice players with sandboxes where they can experience the game through introductory level activities in low-risk environments conducive to experimentation. The skills as strategies principle describes the phenomenon whereby people are motivated to learn and practice skills by viewing these activities as a strategy to achieve their goals. Computer games realize this principle, as their design requires players to learn and practice skills. Players perceive the skills they acquire during play as a means for accomplishing their in-game goals.

The category of "understanding" encompasses the principles of "system thinking," and "meaning as action image." The system thinking principle reflects the view that learning is supported when learners are able to conceptualize their activities as part of a larger complex system that encourages and restricts certain behaviors. Good games reflect this principle when they require players to undertake training activities that enhance understanding of the game as a whole. Meaning as action image, describes the claim that learning occurs through meaningful experience and actions in the world, and that these are stored in the mind as simulations. Computer games make the meaning of words and concepts clear through experiences and activities that are directly tied to action. They enable players to build a repertoire of simulations in the mind that prepare them for future situated action.

Although Gee's research does not focus specifically on the relationship between participation in computer gaming and language acquisition, his work has touched upon this area. In a recent unpublished manuscript during discussion of the information on demand and just in time principle, Gee asserts that as computer games enable language to be situated they may facilitate language learning:

> Since video games are "action-and-goal-directed preparations for, and simulations of, embodied experience" they allow language to be put into the context of dialogue, experience, images, and actions. They allow language to be situated. Furthermore, good video games give verbal information "just in time"—near the time it can actually be used—or "on demand"—when the player feels a need for it and is ready for it (Gee 2003). They don't give players lots and lots of words out of context before they can be used and experienced or before they are needed or useful. *This is an ideal situation for language acquisition* (Italics added), for acquiring new words and new forms of language for new types of activity, whether this be being a member of a SWAT team or a scientist of a certain sort." (Gee 2011, 17)

Computer Games and Learning: The Literacy Perspective

Scholars have increasingly turned their attention to understanding the new forms of literacy made possible by the emergence of digital technologies (Lankshear and Knobel 2006). This body of work is diverse, and encompasses a wide range of theoretical perspectives (Coiro 2003; Lankshear 1997; Leu 2001; Street 2003). An important area of this research explores the enhanced opportunities for human development made possible by the rise of the Internet and associated communication tools (Jenkins 2006; Kress

2003). Researchers in this area frequently draw on sociocultural accounts of literacy, which contest the formally dominant psychological view. For these researchers, literacy is primarily a sociocultural rather than a psychological phenomenon. In contrast to the psychological approach that emphasizes the central role of individual mental processes, researchers who adopt the sociocultural perspective argue for a broader conception of literacy. Literacy is conceived as a complex phenomenon that encompasses more than the ability to read and write. A central claim is that literacy now takes a variety of forms and should be understood in its full range of contexts. Moreover, it is conceptualized as a social and cultural achievement that is deeply embedded in the distinct social, historical, and cultural practices of groups and communities. In this view, digital tools such as computer games possess properties similar to language, as they provide a means to communicate meaning and enact the social relationships (Kist 2004) that are crucial in fostering literacy development. A number of researchers who adopt this perspective have conceptualized computer games as a new form of literacy, and have investigated how games may facilitate human learning (Gerber 2009; Sanford and Madill 2007). An exemplar of this approach can be found in the work of Steinkuehler (2004, 2006, 2007, 2008a, 2008b) who has conducted a series of studies into the new form of literacy and educational possibilities created by the emergence of Internet-based role-playing games.

In a series of papers, Steinkuehler has undertaken a comprehensive examination of the in-game and game-related activities of players in MMORPGs. This work has been conducted using the analytical tools of cognitive ethnography (Hutchins 1995) and discourse analysis (Gee 1999). Steinkuehler provides the following rationale for her research:

> Such games are ripe for cultural/cognitive analysis of the social and material practices attending them: Given their increasing domination of the entertainment industry, wide-spread and growing popularity with people of all age groups, ethnicities, and economic classes, and purported addictive quality of those who plug in...MMOGs are quickly becoming the form of entertainment and a major mechanism of socialization for young and old alike. (Steinkuehler 2004, 521)

For Steinkuehler (2006, 40), the rich virtual worlds provided by MMORPGs that blend fantasy elements with realism and a strong narrative element are an important social phenomenon that is non-trivial and requires investigation. Steinkuehler's analysis focuses on two interrelated areas: the literacy practices of gamers, and their use of language both during gameplay and in game-related chat rooms, fan web sites, mailing lists, blogs, and discussion forums.

A focus of Steinkuehler's work is the study of language-in-use. The examination of this feature of player activity is of importance, as it provides insights into the human relationships that play a key role in learning and literacy development in games:

> Language-in-use functions not only as a vehicle for conveying information but also, and equally important, as part and parcel of *ongoing activities* and as a means for *enacting human relationships*. (Steinkuehler 2006, 39)

For Steinkuehler (2006, 42) the in-game language produced by gamers is a form of hybrid writing that includes the frequent use of abbreviations, truncations, specialized vocabulary, typographical, and syntactic errors. This researcher argues that although this form of writing appears limited it:

> serves the same range and complexity of functions as language does offline. (Steinkuehler 2007, 303)

As table 3.3 shows, Steinkuehler (2007, 302) further identifies a number of specific in-game and out-of-game literacy practices elicited by MMORPGs. In-game practices include the titling of player avatars, letter writing, the delivery of detailed narratives, meeting holding conventions, rituals, the coordination of joint expeditions, and sports. She also draws attention to out-of-game metagaming literacy practices (Steinkuehler 2007, 308). This term refers to the game-related discussions conducted by members of game

Table 3.3 Steinkuehler's factors involved in learning and literacy development in MMORPGs

Factor	Manifestation
Digital media literacy practices (in-game)	In-game text talk, letter writing, orally delivered narratives, meeting holding conventions, titling of avatars, rituals, coordination of joint expeditions, sports
Digital media literacy practices (out-of-game)	Discussion of game strategies, models of performance, theorizing over game norms
Collaboration	Problem solving, feedback, scaffolding
Scientific reasoning	Hypothesis testing, model-based reasoning
Computation literacy	Modding
Cultural mechanisms for learning	Apprenticeships

communities in such venues as online forums, messages boards, and fan websites. These include the discussion of in-game strategies, the development of mathematical models designed to enhance in-game performance, and theorizing over game norms. Steinkuehler concludes, based on a comprehensive analysis of data collected over a two-year period, that these games are a form of literacy activity (Steinkuehler 2007, 301). She asserts that they provide access to communities of practice, where players can gain knowledge and learn skills through in and out-of-game meaning-based collaborative interactions with other players (Steinkuehler 2007, 300). These interactions frequently involve overcoming complex challenges through problem solving (Steinkuehler 2008b). For this researcher, collaborative activity involving social interaction is the distinguishing feature of this type of game and is essential for player success (Steinkuehler 2006, 47). During gameplay and in beyond-game venues players read and write copious amounts of text relating to the game. At the same time, they learn how to advance in the game hierarchy by mastering specific skills through sustained interaction with peers. This involves the provision of feedback and scaffolding. Scientific reasoning is also developed through hypothesis testing and model-based reasoning. During this apprenticeship process players are not only learning, they are at the same time socialized into shared game-based community values and goals (Steinkuehler 2006, 47). They further develop their computational literacy through adapting existing games, a process known as "modding" (Steinkuehler 2008b). The creation of personally meaningful artifacts during this activity assists in the development of gaming literacy skills (Salen 2007).

In Steinkuehler's view, MMORPGs represent a new form of literacy and constitute cultural mechanisms for learning (Steinkuehler 2006, 2008b). Echoing claims made by other researchers (Shaffer et al. 2005), she asserts that the activities engendered by gameplay and participation in game-related social communities facilitate the development of the literacy skills that are essential for success in the network-based globalized society of the twenty-first century. For Steinkuehler, there is a need to investigate the nature of MMORPGs, in order to establish design principles that may be usefully applied in other learning environments, and in education more generally (Steinkuehler 2008b).

Research on Computer Games and Learning

The theoretical work discussed in this chapter has stimulated research conducted in a variety of contexts, and from a range of theoretical perspectives, that explores the phenomenon of computer gaming. Researchers draw attention to the expansion in research studies that focus on computer games (O'Neil, Wainess, and Baker 2005, 461). However, as has been noted in the literature, publications that investigate the relationship between computer games and human learning remain relatively limited (Mitchell and Savill-Smith 2004). Nonetheless, researchers have conducted meta-analyses. The discussion in this section investigates significant findings from these studies. In order to provide historical perspective, and to facilitate the identification of common patterns in the literature, meta-analyses were selected that reflect the findings of significant research conducted since the 1970s. Moreover, the findings of large-scale meta-analyses that focus specifically on investigating the educational possibilities presented by computer games are analyzed.

An early meta-analysis conducted by Randel et al. (1992) examined studies that compared the instructional effectiveness of computer games to conventional classroom environments. The researchers analyzed the findings of 67 studies conducted over 28 years until 1991. These involved the following areas: social sciences, math, physics, biology, logic, and language arts. Results of the analysis indicate that the majority of the studies (46) focused on the social sciences, and that, of the studies as a whole, 56 percent found no difference in student performance between games and conventional classroom instruction. A minority of the studies (32 percent) found differences favoring games. Moreover, 7 percent of the studies explicitly favored games. However, the controls used in this latter set of papers are problematic. The findings indicate that games appear more effective in areas such as math, physics, and language arts where content can be targeted and objectives defined. In the area of retention, studies suggest that participation in computer gaming induces greater retention over time than conventional instructional approaches. Another significant finding across the studies was that students consistently report they find games to be more interesting than regular classes. The researchers identify a number of issues with the research designs adopted in the majority of the papers. For example, the reliability and validity of tests used to measure effectiveness were often not reported. Few of the studies were longitudinal, and, frequently, important issues such as teacher bias, sample selection, and novelty were not considered. Moreover, in the majority of studies researchers seldom considered variables that have a major influence on learning such as personality, debriefing, academic, and game ability.

De Aguilera and Mendiz (2003) explored the findings of studies conducted over a twenty-year period until 2003. The above researchers note that in early research there was a tendency in many studies to focus exclusively on the perceived negative effects of video games on children. They claim that although this trend has continued, findings do not support this contention, and that contemporary research has produced conflicting results:

> After two decades, research results on video games are somewhat confusing. First, the disciplinary and methodological approaches on which these studies were based vary. Second, the effects of video games were measured using parameters (i.e., types of games, platforms, age groups, length of exposure) that are not always comparable. And last, the research is fragmented, inconclusive, and barely consistent with any multidisciplinary outlook that embraces the sciences of psychology, psychiatry, education, sociology, and communications. Despite attempts to demonstrate that video games have a pernicious influence on players, there is no scientific evidence to support this claim. To the contrary, some positive effects, particularly those of an instructive nature, have proven to be more empirically and theoretically evident. (De Aguilera and Mendiz 2003, 3)

These researchers assert that although varying in approach, the consensus among more recent studies is that computer games are motivating and can support the development of a number of skills involved in learning. Skills identified from the literature analyzed by De Aguilera and Mendiz include reading, logical thinking, observation, basic knowledge, problem solving, decision-making, and strategic planning. The above researchers identify certain types of computer games as having the potential to facilitate the development of specific skills. Puzzle and question games are claimed to support the development of logical thinking, while simulation games can support intellectual development. They further note that strategy and role-playing games enhance motivation and reflection on game values. Finally, the beneficial effects of playing arcade and console games are identified as enhancing psychomotor coordination, spatial orientation, and stress reduction.

A comprehensive meta-analysis of research on games reported by Hays (2005) examined the findings of 105 articles. These include 26 review articles, 31 theoretical articles, and 48 articles that provided empirical data on the effectiveness of instructional gaming, including the use of computer games. This study identifies mixed results and highlights a number of problematic issues. Hays observes that

> the empirical research on the effectiveness of instructional games is fragmented. (Hays 2005, 6)

This researcher draws attention to the wide range of games, age groups, and tasks that have been investigated. Hays suggests that this feature of the literature hampers systematic research efforts. In negative findings, he draws attention to the problem of ill-defined terminology and further highlights widespread methodological issues with many of the studies. Problematic areas include limited use of random sampling, lack of control groups, the absence of pre- and posttest measurement of performance gains, and problematic questionnaire design. As a result of these issues, and the absence of any discussion of methodology in some studies, Hays claims that findings are frequently difficult to generalize. Hays further asserts that there is no evidence to indicate that games are the preferred method of instruction in every educational context. In a positive finding, he emphasizes that some games including computer games, do provide effective learning. He also highlights areas where learning can be enhanced, such as providing instructional support and embedding the game in an instructional program.

O'Neil, Wainess, and Baker (2005) analyzed the findings of empirical studies that investigated video games and learning outcomes for adults. These researchers analyzed 19 peer-reviewed articles conducted over a period of 15 years that provided either qualitative or quantitative perspectives on effectiveness. Analysis of these studies produced both positive and negative findings. These researchers emphasize the educational potential of computer games, and the limited extent of empirical evidence:

> The evidence of potential is striking, but the empirical evidence for the effectiveness of games as learning environments is scant. (O'Neil, Wainess, and Baker 2005, 468)

In common with other meta-analyses, the above researchers draw attention to limitations of the research designs used in many of the studies. They note that in the majority of the studies they examined, only a single measure was used to investigate learning. Only five studies used multiple measures. Few studies examine important areas such as content understanding. Although several papers investigate collaboration, none of them attempted to measure this phenomenon. Areas identified as playing a major role in learning such as, for example, self-regulation, were not investigated. The above researchers claimed that the majority of studies focused solely on problem solving. They suggest that this situation is problematic as there is evidence in the literature that questions the effectiveness of this approach in instruction. Based on their analysis, the researchers emphasize the importance of embedding computer games in an appropriate context and assert that

> our position is that games themselves are not sufficient for learning, but there are elements in games that can be activated within an instructional context that may enhance the learning process. (Ibid., 465)

They further claim that in order for computer games to support learning they must incorporate sound instructional design principles combined with measures that reduce cognitive load. In the view of these researchers, computer games will be more effective learning tools when they combine learning supports such as worked examples, and various forms of scaffolding including feedback, hints, prompts, and graphic organizers.

Dondlinger (2007) carried out a meta-analysis of 35 peer-reviewed papers produced over a 10-year period that examined theoretical rationales for game design, the identification of design elements conducive to learning, and learning outcomes from video gameplay. In terms of beneficial learning outcomes, the analysis indicates that the majority of papers contain claims that computer games facilitate learning. A consistent theme of the above literature is that computer games elicit a high degree of motivation. However, there is disagreement regarding its source. Four studies identify narrative context as a significant factor in motivating players. In contrast, eight papers contain claims that goals, rules, and rewards are responsible for the high degree of motivation engendered. In five papers researchers identify the interactivity and multisensory cues provided by computer games as supporting immersion, collaboration, and learning. Dondlinger identifies nine papers where it is claimed that playing computer games supports the development of deductive reasoning, hypothesis testing, and deep learning. Moreover, five of the above studies report findings that suggest mastery of complex abstract and conceptual knowledge is facilitated by participation in computer gaming. Two studies emphasize the enhanced opportunities for the development of visual and spatial processing.

A recent meta-analysis of research on the educational effectiveness of serious games across a variety of domains, undertaken by Wouters, Spek, and Oostendorp (2009), reports significant findings. These researchers analyzed 28 empirical studies conducted in the ten years prior to 2008. The analysis reveals a number of both positive and negative findings. The majority of studies show that the use of serious games appears to promote cognitive and motor skills. The analysis suggests that serious games improve the acquisition of new knowledge. The positive attitudes engendered are identified as a benefit. In terms of communicative learning outcomes, the above literature contains evidence that the type of task and the specific game type employed may influence this factor. However, the above researchers acknowledge that research on the effects of serious games on other aspects of communication skills remains limited. The analysis revealed little direct evidence to support the contention that serious games enhance motivation. In a further significant finding, the researchers emphasized that without adequate support, many learners may face cognitive overload as playing serious games is a complex and cognitively demanding activity. The researchers emphasize the limited nature of research that specifically addresses the impact of important variables on learner performance such as, gender, training, and age. They further stress the importance of assessment issues. The above researchers conclude their work by drawing attention to the potential of serious games while emphasizing the necessity for further research.

The findings of the meta-analyses examined in this discussion draw attention to a number of recurrent themes identified in the literature on computer games and learning. A number of positive findings are emphasized. The work conducted by De Aguilera and Mendiz (2003), Dondlinger (2007), and Randel et al. (1992), draws attention to research conducted in a wide range of settings, suggesting that computer games are highly motivating and interesting for learners. These findings lend some support to the claims of game theorists (Crawford 1984; Prensky 2002) who have long argued that a major benefit of using computer games in education is the high degree of motivation and interest they elicit. Another encouraging finding identified in the above work is the beneficial effects that participation in computer gaming appears to have on the development of cognitive skills associated with learning. In their analysis of the literature, De Aguilera and Mendiz (2003) and Dondlinger (2007) emphasize evidence suggesting that frequent use of computer games supports enhanced literacy and problem-solving skills. Wouters, Spek, and Oostendorp (2009) and the above researchers note consistent evidence for improved visualization and psychomotor skills. These findings provide evidence to support assertions made by theorists of literacy and learning who advocate the use of computer games in education (Gee 2007a, Steinkuehler 2008a). O'Neil, Wainess, and Baker (2005); Wouters, Spek, and Oostendorp (2009); and Hays (2005), further suggest that in formal educational contexts the potential of computer games can be significantly improved, through the provision of learning support, and close integration with the instructional program in which they are used.

The findings of the meta-analyses analyzed in this section further highlight a number of significant issues with the current body of research on computer games and learning. Hays (2005) while acknowledging that the number of papers is expanding rapidly, draws attention to the limited number of studies that specifically address learners' actual game experiences. In common with other researchers (Mitchell and Savill-Smith 2004; Randel et al. 1992; Whitton 2010), Hays notes a long-running characteristic of the literature, namely, the prevalence of anecdotal small-scale research. O'Neil, Wainess, and Baker (2005, 462) claim it is essential that more empirical peer-reviewed research on computer games and learning outcomes is carried out as, although some research suggests that participation in computer gaming may be beneficial, many studies make unsupported claims. Moreover, a number of important areas remain poorly understood and have yet to be the subject of extensive research (Anderson and Bushman 2001). Researchers have also identified a number of methodological problems that appear widespread in current research (Griffiths 1996; Harris 2001). Echoing concerns voiced elsewhere in the literature, Randel et al. (1992) and O'Neil, Wainess, and Baker (2005) emphasize that many papers lack adequate controls, and rely on only a single measure of learning. This makes their results difficult to generalize. These researchers further draw attention to the limited number of rigorous longitudinal studies and that research frequently fails to explore the influence of important variables such as, for example, attitudes. In terms of investigating learning outcomes, Wouters, Spek, and Oostendorp (2009) highlight the need to develop new assessment methods that take account of the particular contexts provided by computer games.

This chapter has investigated early research that explored the relationship between computer games and learning. The discussion has examined contemporary theoretical work conducted by researchers in the fields of game studies, literacy, and digital media that has attempted to identify the features of computer games that may be involved in facilitating human learning. This chapter has further analyzed the literature that explores the relationship between participation in computer gaming and learning outcomes. The analysis has revealed evidence indicating that computer gaming may support factors associated with learning. However, the discussion has acknowledged that current learner-based research is limited in scope, and subject to a number of methodological limitations. Although the research analyzed in this chapter is useful in providing a context to better comprehend the potential benefits of computer games as educational tools, it has not, for the most part, focused specifically on language learning. The following chapter will explore influential theories of language learning and examines rationales proposed for the use of computer games in language education that draw on this theoretical work.

CHAPTER 4

Computer Games and Language Learning: Theoretical Rationales

This chapter explores theories of SLA and their influence on the field of CALL. The discussion highlights the diverse nature of theories proposed in the literature, and examines accounts of foreign language learning that may be relevant to learning with computer games. Elements of cognitive conceptualizations of SLA are explored, as are more recent constructs drawn from research that is informed by theories that stress the social nature of language acquisition. It is observed that SLA research is subject to limitations, and that there is, at present, no consensus regarding a generally accepted theory. Nonetheless, evidence suggests that both of the above accounts provide insights into the complex nature of SLA. Moreover, it is asserted that these conceptualizations are valuable, as they identify many of the conditions in which SLA may occur. The discussion then turns to investigate research that has explored the relationship between the above theories and CALL. The discussion emphasizes that the SLA theories were not devised to account for learning in computer-based environments. However, research indicates that elements of the above accounts may be relevant to understanding language learning in computer-based environments. This chapter then examines theoretical rationales that draw on elements of SLA theory in order to justify the use of computer games in CALL. The value of these pioneering efforts is acknowledged. Although the rationales are provisional in nature, the discussion shows that they highlight the potential of computer games to facilitate language learning, and provide a credible framework to guide future development work.

SLA Theory and CALL

In the postwar era, research on human learning was heavily influenced by behaviorist psychology. This conceptualized learning as, at a fundamental level, solely an inner mental phenomenon that is the product of responses to external stimuli. In terms of the influence of behaviorism on classroom learning the work of Skinner (1954, 1968) was highly influential in the 1950s and 1960s. Skinner (1957) emphasized that languages could be learned through conditioning. He claimed that, through participation in repetitive drills involving mimicry, reinforcement, and memorization, learning could be facilitated. This approach was reflected in the development of the programmed instruction movement. As was noted in chapter 1, this promoted the use of computers as instructional tools, and greatly influenced language education including early CALL research. Although the influence of behaviorism on language teaching and CALL has continued, the limitations of this approach were highlighted in the literature. By the early 1980s, new theories of learning emerged, that drew attention to the limitations of behaviorism and emphasized that human cognition was a far more complex phenomenon than was previously thought. This development had a profound effect on the field of SLA. Moreover, this new theoretical work was reflected in the development at this time of communicative CALL, a movement that, as Warschauer and Healy note:

> stressed that computer-based activities should focus on using forms rather than on the forms themselves, teach grammar implicitly rather than implicitly, allow and encourage students to generate original utterances rather than just manipulate prefabricated language, and use the target language predominately or even exclusively. (Warschauer and Healy 1998, 58)

As new views of learning become more widespread, theory development in SLA expanded rapidly. By the early 1990s, numerous theories of SLA had emerged as Larson-Freeman and Long observe:

> There are at least forty claims, arguments, theories, and perspectives that attempt to describe and explain the learning process and predict its outcomes. (Larsen-Freeman and Long 1991, 227)

This situation was welcomed by contemporary CALL researchers such as Garret (1991), who noted the need for new theories in order to better comprehend the opportunities for language learning made possible by developments in computer technologies. The emergence of the Internet and powerful low-cost computers in the 1990s has contributed, in part, to a significant increase in CALL research. This phenomenon continues to the present day. Moreover, the expansion in SLA theory development has continued at an increasing pace (Bardovi-Harlig and Dörnyei 2006; Mitchell and Myles 2004). However, as was noted previously, the technology-driven nature of much development work in CALL remains a constant theme in the literature. As was observed in chapter 1, this situation requires a theory-led approach to the use and evaluation of new technologies in language education. In this context, theorists have emphasized the benefits of linking CALL research to developments in closely related fields such as SLA:

> Situating CALL research and practice within well-defined or established theoretical and methodological frameworks is a way to bring coherence to a field that is sometimes perceived as lacking in focus and direction. (Levy 2000, 170)

Although researchers draw attention to the continuing debates in the literature over the nature of SLA (Lafford 2007; Tarone 2007), and emphasize that this body of work was not originally developed to account for language learning with computers, they nonetheless highlight the value of applying the findings of SLA research to CALL (Chapelle 1997, 2004; Doughty 1987). In an example of this phenomenon, Chapelle has recently stated that

> the pragmatic goal of computer-assisted language learning (CALL) developers and researchers to create and evaluate learning opportunities pushes them to consider a variety of theoretical approaches to second language acquisition. (Chapelle 2009, 741)

Researchers have argued that two main strands of SLA theory may be of relevance to development work involving the use of new computer-based technologies in CALL (Chapelle 2009; Salaberry 1999), and it is to a brief overview of these accounts that the discussion will now turn.

Accounts of SLA Relevant to CALL

Of the many theories put forward to explain SLA cognitive approaches constitute the mainstream view (Lafford 2007). Cognitive theories of SLA focus on the individual and view language learning as a process that occurs in the mind of the learner (Long 1990). A common theme in many of these theories is the claim that second or foreign language acquisition is the product of innate mental processes (Kasper 1997). Researchers who adopt this perspective use quantitative research methods in order to investigate the mental processes at work in SLA (Gregg 1993). Additional factors identified as significant include the role of mental and linguistic variables on language processing and development (Ellis 1984; Long 1997; Pienemann 2007). A number of influential constructs are proposed in the body of work that constitutes the cognitive account of SLA. In the input hypothesis, exposure to comprehensible TL input is emphasized, and affective factors are perceived as influencing learning (Krashen 1977, 1981, 1982, 1985, 2003). In the interaction hypothesis (Long 1996), it is claimed that learning is facilitated when learners engage in TL interaction involving negotiation of meaning (Pica 1994; Varonis and Gass 1985). Additional factors identified as significant in cognitive accounts of SLA include conscious awareness (Fotos 1993; Robinson 1995), including noticing (Schmidt 1990, 1992), and the mental process involved in the production of comprehensible TL output (Swain 1985, 1995; Swain and Lapkin 1995).

An alternative conception of language learning to that proposed by cognitive research can be found in the work of researchers who stress the social nature of the cognition involved in language learning (Tarone 2007). These researchers criticize cognitive accounts of SLA for ignoring or downplaying the influence of contextual factors (Foster 1998; Lafford 2007). From this perspective, language use and acquisition are perceived as inherently social phenomena (Atkinson 2002). Proponents of this view argue for an expanded conception of SLA in which language learning is seen as a dynamic social process in which interaction, collaboration, and contextual factors play a central role (Firth and Wagner 2007). Researchers who adopt this view use qualitative research methods in order to explore language learning. Influential concepts in this body of work draw, in part, on ideas first developed by Vygotsky (1978) such as mediation, regulation, private speech, and zones of proximal development (DiCamilla and Anton 2004; Donato 1994; Lantolf 2000; Lantolf and Appel 1994; Lantolf and Thorne 2006; Ohta 2000; Wertsch 2007). Other related constructs that are also proposed in accounts of SLA that emphasize the social and community-based nature of learning include language socialization (Ochs and Schieffelin 1995; Watson-Gegeo and Neilson 2003; Zuengler and Miller 2006), and situated learning theory (Lave 1988; Mondada and Doehler 2004; Swain and Deters 2007; Wenger 1998).

CALL researchers claim (Chapelle 2009; Salaberry 1999; Thorne 2008) that there is evidence in the literature indicating that although SLA research is subject to limitations, it is valuable, as it identifies many of the conditions in which language acquisition may occur. Moreover, they assert that a considerable body of CALL research informed by cognitive and social SLA, indicates that these accounts are relevant to understanding how learning may be facilitated through the use of computer technologies (Al-Seghayer 2001; Blake 2000; Darhower 2002, Fernandez-Garcia and Martinez-Arbelaiz 2002; Jepson 2005; Kim 2011; Kötter 2003; Lee 2008; Lomicka 1998; Plass et al. 1998; Shin 2006; Smith 2003; Von Der Emde, Schneider, and Kötter 2001; Yanguas 2009; Yoshii 2006). In this context, researchers have drawn on concepts articulated in SLA theory to propose rationales for the use of computer games in CALL.

Rationales for the Use of Computer Games in CALL

As Chapelle (2009, 748) observes, assessing the potential of new technologies in CALL requires the development of robust theoretically based conceptual and evaluative frameworks. In the context of conceptualizing the potential of computer games as tools for language learning, researchers have drawn on SLA research in order to propose a number of theoretical rationales to guide research and development work. The discussion in this section examines these efforts.

An Early Rationale

García-Carbonell et al. (2001) made one of the first attempts to justify the use of computer games in language education. As may be observed in table 4.1, these researchers propose a rationale for the use of computer games based on cognitive SLA and gaming theory. Drawing on gaming theory, they argue that the rule-based competitive nature of gaming stimulates factors associated with SLA including enhanced learner activity, teamwork, experimentation, and motivation. This rationale is based, in part, on the assertion that as many well-designed computer games provide for interaction with peers, they maximize learner exposure to the comprehensible input identified in cognitive accounts of SLA (Krashen 1982). The above researchers claim that as games provide for learner-centered rather than teacher-led interaction they elicit the production of TL output. Another related benefit of participation in gaming identified in this rationale are the opportunities to engage in authentic interaction involving the negotiation of meaning, that is held to promote language learning in cognitive SLA research (Ellis 1984). The above researchers further claim that computer-based games are an effective means to enhance the development of the communicative competence as they require purposeful goal-directed TL interaction involving the types

Table 4.1 A rationale for the use of computer games in CALL García-Carbonell et al. (2001)

Gaming feature(s)	Hypothesized benefit(s)	Theoretical justification
Rules Competition	Learner activity stimulated Teamwork Experimentation Enhanced motivation	Gaming research
Purposeful TL interaction involving tasks	Opportunities to negotiate meaning Development of communicative competence	Cognitive and interactionist SLA research
Computer-based learner-centered interaction	Exposure to comprehensible input Learner-centered interaction Production of TL output Influence of factors that may inhibit learning reduced	Cognitive SLA research

of collaborative task that are identified as beneficial in interactionist SLA research. Moreover, it is proposed that participation in computer-based gaming can reduce the influence of affective factors, such as anxiety, that may inhibit learning in many teacher-centered classrooms.

Contemporary Rationales

In a recent paper Thorne, Black, and Sykes (2009) have proposed a rationale to justify the use of a particular genre of computer game in CALL. They argue that from the perspective of sociocultural SLA research, MMORPGs offer a number of potential benefits as venues for language learning. These researchers identify the social nature of interaction in MMORPGs as the primary driver of learning. They draw on language socialization and situated learning theory perspectives to support their claims (Duff 2007; Lave and Wenger 1991). As table 4.2 shows, according to this rationale, the complex, competitive, and engaging nature of the interaction in this genre of computer game is seen as stimulating TL use. Moreover, the goal-directed nature of in-game activities that become progressively more challenging, such as trading and quests, coupled to the need to obtain assistance from other players and non-player agents in order to complete game tasks, leads to

Table 4.2 A rationale for the use of MMORPGs Thorne, Black, and Sykes (2009)

Gaming feature(s)	Hypothesized benefit(s)	Theoretical justification
Challenging and engaging goal-directed TL interaction	Opportunities for TL use	Language socialization theory
	Participation in TL social interaction	
	Peer assistance and instruction	
Membership of in-game social groups	Membership of communities of practice	Situated learning theory
	Learners gradually socialized into game TL norms	
	Establishment and maintenance of collaborative social relationships	

the formation of both short-term and long-term game-based social organizations. Membership of in-game social organizations such as guilds, essential for character progression in the game, is perceived as facilitating acceptance into communities of practice characterized by the provision of peer assistance and instruction. Through active participation in these online groups, learners gradually develop expertise and ultimately achieve legitimate peripheral participation as they are socialized into game community TL norms. This rationale asserts that the above features of gameplay in MMORPGs are reflected in the high frequency of socioemotional talk generated, and the considerable efforts made by players to establish, and maintain, collaborative social relationships that are reported in the literature.

An alternative rationale to justify the use of MMORPGs in language education has been put forward by Zhao and Lai (2009). These researchers support the claim made by Thorne, Black, and Sykes (2009) that, of the computer games currently available, MMORPGs hold the greatest potential as arenas for language learning. However, Zhao and Lai assert that as the amount of social interaction varies significantly between games, purpose-built MMORPGs are more effective for language learning, as they can be designed to provide access to optimal conditions for SLA. They propose a rationale that draws on both social and cognitive accounts of SLA. In terms of cognitive SLA, as table 4.3 shows, these researchers argue that a major advantage of MMORPGs is the access they provide to diverse groups of

Table 4.3 A rationale for the use of MMORPGs Zhao and Lai (2009)

Gaming feature(s)	Hypothesized benefit(s)	Theoretical justification
Access to diverse groups of interlocutors	Comprehensible TL input	Cognitive SLA
Opportunities for authentic TL use	Meaning-focused interaction	
Learner-centered interaction	Opportunities for noticing and negotiation of meaning	
Exposure to real-time feedback		
Access to mediating tools	Scaffolding Mentoring	Sociocultural SLA
Collaborative social interaction	Reduced anxiety	
Participation in in-game and out-of-game communities	Enhanced social cohesion and motivation	

interlocutors that are frequently unavailable in many language classrooms. They further claim that in contrast to much of the content that is available to learners on the Internet, this type of game supplies abundant amounts of rich, stimulating, and comprehensible TL input. In addition, there are ample opportunities for meaning-focused TL use in a context that is more authentic, and purposeful, than that found in many educational settings. In their rationale, Zhao and Lai emphasize that the input provided in this game genre frequently incorporates the type of real-time feedback that supports noticing and negotiation of meaning. Moreover, the learner-centered nature of interaction is seen as promoting individual learning.

Zhao and Lai (2009) further claim that social accounts of SLA particularly those originating in sociocultural theory, can also contribute to a convincing and comprehensive rationale for the use of MMORPGs. The above researchers note that many MMORPGs are specifically designed to facilitate social interaction in TL. Furthermore, these games offer access to mediating tools and offer opportunities for players to participate in both in-game and game-related online communities. They assert that these features of MMORPGs promote types of collaborative interaction that are hypothesized as beneficial in sociocultural SLA. They emphasize the opportunities for scaffolding and mentoring that arise during the joint problem solving that is a central element of play in this type of game. They further observe that repeated exposure to collaborative interaction reduces anxiety and enhances social cohesion. These aspects of gameplay foster the development of a supportive learning environment and the motivation that plays an important role in language learning.

The theoretical rationales examined in this discussion highlight the potential of computer games in CALL. The pioneering work of García-Carbonell et al. (2001) first demonstrated the relevance of game and SLA theory as sources to guide development work. These researchers identify concepts from cognitive SLA research including exposure to comprehensible input, and opportunities for TL interaction, as major advantages of computer games. As this discussion shows, influenced by this early research Thorne, Black, and Sykes (2009) have argued for the use of commercial MMORPGs drawing on a language socialization view of SLA. Zhao and Lai (2009) claim that from the perspective of both cognitive and social accounts of SLA purpose-built games such as MMORPGs are potentially valuable arenas for language learning. Although the rationales proposed differ in theoretical approach, the above researchers assert that this genre of computer game appears to offer many of the optimal conditions for learning that have been identified in SLA research. Moreover, as Zhao and Lai observe, the case for the use of MMORPGs in CALL appears compelling, as this type of game provides many of the above conditions that are frequently challenging to replicate in many traditional language classrooms.

Thorne, Black, and Sykes (2009) identify another important advantage of online games such as MMORPGs, namely, they provide a venue for learning that is free from the traditional constraints of time and distance. Furthermore, these researchers emphasize that young language learners have utilized the development of communications technologies, and the vast expansion of the Internet, to engage in new forms of online communication that involve a wide array of digitally mediated practices. They echo claims in the literature (Lafford 2007) that these developments have given language learners access to new out-of-school environments where language learning can occur. These researchers contend that the international online communities provided by network-based games such as MMORPGs, have created new digital vernaculars that frequently incorporate English has a lingua franca. They argue these games provide alternative venues for a powerful form of participatory learning that involves identity exploration and language socialization meeting needs that are not met in current educational practices. Although the above researchers acknowledge that studies on the use of MMORPGs are limited in number and scope, they nonetheless make a convincing case for additional research on the use of this particular genre of game in CALL.

In accordance with the argument made in chapter 1, that stresses the need to link CALL research to theories of language learning, this chapter has examined influential constructs and theories proposed to account for SLA. The discussion has emphasized that while these theories are subject to continuing debate, elements of both cognitive and social accounts of language learning appear to provide insights that are of value in identifying the conditions in which the complex process of SLA may occur. This chapter has shown that current SLA theories were not developed to account for learning in computer-based environments. However, the discussion draws attention to evidence in the literature indicating that SLA theories are of relevance to CALL. The CALL research analyzed here suggests that theories of input and interaction hypothesized in both main strands of SLA research can be usefully applied to CALL evaluation and development work. In this context, the discussion has analyzed rationales for the use of computer games in CALL that are based on SLA theory. Although these rationales differ in theoretical emphasis and are provisional, they are nonetheless valuable, as they highlight many features of participation in computer gaming that appear beneficial for second language learning. The contemporary rationales examined in this chapter emphasize that of the computer games currently available, MMORPGs appear particularly promising. Moreover, these rationales offer the advantage of providing a robust conceptual theoretical framework to guide development work that explores the use of this type of game. The emergence of the rationales examined in this discussion highlights the need for detailed investigation of learner-based research on the use of computer games in CALL. The findings of this body of work will be analyzed in the following chapters.

CHAPTER 5

Early Research on the Use of Computer Games in CALL: An Overview

Computer Games in Language Education: Early Work

Primitive computer games first emerged in the 1950's (Kirriemuir and McFarlane 2004). However, it was the development of mainframe computers that initiated the first large-scale research on the use of computer games in education (R. Sanders 1995). As was noted in chapter 1, the development of PLATO led to work that explored the use of this system in language education (Hart 1995). Games were incorporated in several PLATO systems designed for language learning, and several descriptions of this work are reported in the literature. In an example of this approach, Cole, Lebowitz, and Hart (1981) reported on the use of PLATO-based versions of popular classroom word games, such as tic-tac-toe, in a system designed to teach Hebrew. In a system for the study of Russian, Hart and Provenzano (1973) described a vocabulary learning game called concentration in which learners match Russian words with their English equivalents. The system recorded responses in order to enable learners to compare their scores with other players. Positive learner feedback to PLATO language games (Grundlehner 1974), coupled to the emergence of low-cost microcomputers and accessible programming languages, stimulated interest in the use of computer games in CALL. As these technologies advanced, computer games became an increasing focus of research (Philips 1987) and were viewed as a technology with great potential (Hubbard 1991). Work focused on two main areas. The first area of interest involved use of text-manipulation games that enable learners to engage in gap filling or reordering of various types of TL sentences or texts (Hewer 1997). The second area of investigation focused on the use of text-based adventure games that immerse the player in a computer-based virtual world described in text and on-screen graphics (Baltra 1984). The following discussion will examine studies on the above game types that have been described in chapter 2. In order to identify significant early studies from the period 1980 through 1999, a database search was conducted of the main CALL journals: *ReCALL, System, CALICO Journal, Language Learning & Technology, CALL Journal*, and this revealed five studies. An expanded Internet search produced three studies. The eight studies identified in the above searches were selected for analysis, as they specifically investigate learner use of the above games. The examination of this body of work is necessary, as it offers the prospect of identifying significant early findings on the potential benefits of playing these types of computer games.

The Use of Text-Manipulation Games in CALL

In an early experimental study, Piper (1986) examined learner use of three text-manipulation games. Two gap-filling games and a reordering game were utilized in this research. The researcher videoed three different groups made up of EFL learners from six countries. This research was designed to establish if playing the games would elicit use of beneficial types of TL interaction. Analysis of the video recordings revealed mixed findings. Playing the games generated considerable TL output in the groups with the game *Clozemaster* generating the highest number of turns. Researcher observation confirmed that the learners were highly engaged by the games. Moreover, they displayed behaviors associated with language learning in the sociocultural account of SLA. These behaviors included repeatedly thinking out loud and talking to themselves while playing the games. This finding indicates that the learners were engaging in inner speech. This study further revealed less positive findings. The researcher noted that the learners' TL output was not, for the most part, linguistically rich. Turn lengths elicited by the gameplay were very short, comprising at most a few words, and the use of repetitive sequences was frequent. A variety of TL functions such as agreeing, disagreeing, checking, and contradicting appeared in the data. However, the learner output was characterized by the production of a limited range of language forms and lexis. There was an absence of any evidence that negotiation occurred during learner-learner interaction elicited by the gameplay. Moreover, no instances of self-correction were identified. Piper emphasized the generally impoverished nature of the discourse, and that the conversational spin-off generated by the games was limited. Although this study examined learner linguistic output in great detail, it focused solely on use of the programs in self-access mode. This represents a missed opportunity, as this research did not explore the potential of integrating the games into a regular language course.

Legenhausen and Wolff (1990) reported on exploratory research involving learner classroom use of the *Storyboard* text-reconstruction game. The research was conducted within the framework of a cognitive SLA perspective that emphasizes the importance of the following three mental processes: hypothesis formation, hypothesis testing, and automatization. The above researchers attempted to establish if playing the game would elicit hypothesis formation and testing. Moreover, they claimed that if these mental processes occurred, this would provide evidence for the related process of automatization that is held to play a central role in language learning. Data analysis was conducted based on recording of reconstruction events and verbal reporting. The participants were divided into two groups. One group attempted to reconstruct a text of 103 words without viewing it beforehand. A second group viewed the same text for 30 seconds before they attempted the same task. Both groups were given 20 minutes to play the game. Quantitative analysis of reconstruction attempts showed that both groups made the same number of reconstruction attempts with learners producing on average 52 different words. The second group had a higher success rate in correctly identifying content words scoring 21.04 words compared to the first group's 2.51 words. The first group produced a higher number of function words 28.45 compared to 21.53. However, the second group produced more correct function words.

The researchers observed that the game elicited a high degree of engagement and three types of mental activities were identified: text-independent strategies based on activation of preexisting linguistic knowledge not related to the text, text-dependent strategies that were elicited by participation in the game, and, in the case of the second group, memory strategies. The most common text-dependent strategy was the frequency strategy that contains three subtypes: activation of function words, frequent verbs, and other frequent words. Frequency strategies were more common in the first group. Text-independent strategies were infrequent in both groups. A range of text-dependent problem-solving strategies appeared in the data. The most frequent were grammatical strategies, followed by interpretation strategies, word knowledge strategies, semantic strategies, and textual strategies. The researchers claimed that selection of the above strategies activated both explicit and partially explicit linguistic knowledge. They further asserted that implicit knowledge may have, to a degree, been transferred into explicit knowledge through hypothesis testing during the game. However, they were unable to establish if playing the game facilitates the development of second language (henceforth L2) competences involved in reception and production. They argued that in the absence of purposeful TL interaction, activation of isolated linguistic knowledge may not, in itself, necessarily enhance these competences.

In a classroom-based pilot project, Higgins, Lawrie, and White (1999) examined use of the text-manipulation game *Sequitir*. This game is designed to develop awareness of cohesion devices and coherence features. As was noted in chapter 2, the game displays a short text in which the sentences are in the correct order up to certain point. Learners are invited to select the most appropriate continuation from three alternatives. In the event that an incorrect response is selected it is grayed out and the player is prompted to make a further selection until the text is reconstructed appropriately. The researchers analyzed user logs in order to track learner responses and confirm the amount of time taken in decision-making. Data from three different groups of intermediate-level EFL learners was collected. In the first group, the time taken by each learner was analyzed in order to examine confidence. The data revealed that the learners took longer to answer and scored lower than two native speaker controls. There was a tendency for higher correct responses with slower runs. The most frequent answer pattern made by the learners was a quick wrong answer followed by a slow right answer, followed by a slow wrong answer and a quick right answer. The researchers suggested the former pattern provided evidence of reflection.

In the second group, five learners studying for the IELTS examination played the game. Errors in classroom writing were compared with game responses. The analysis revealed that, when playing the game, participants appeared to experience difficulties also identified in their classroom writing. These focused on the use of connectors, an anaphoric pronoun, and the impersonal it or there. In the final experiment, five native speakers and five learners played the game in an attempt to establish intuitions regarding paragraph structure. The data showed that with two exceptions, participants in both groups experienced difficulties in making the correct choices when reconstructing the text. Moreover, it was found that they made errors at the same point in the game. This finding appeared due to the ambiguous nature of the paragraph that did not conform to the participant's expectations. The researchers claimed that the findings showed the potential of this type of game in the teaching of reading and writing. This research was subject to a number of limitations. The number of participants was limited, and the number of learners in the first group was not specified. Moreover, the first language backgrounds of these learners were not specified in detail.

A major limitation of the research design was the lack of any rationale based on theories of language learning. In preliminary research, Johns and Wang (1999) investigated the use of a later version of the game *Bilingual Sentence Shuffler*. In this game, players must select and then reorder a short English text. A parallel translation of the selected text is provided in Chinese. The game provides access to texts of varying levels of difficulty and utilizes a gambling scoring system that includes a hall of fame feature. In this study, the researchers recorded the verbal interaction of two learners during gameplay. One participant was a native speaker of Chinese; the other was a native speaker of English. Data analysis indicated that both learners found the texts challenging and that they actively assisted each other in completing the game task. The researchers claimed that the learners engaged in reciprocal learning relating to the development of reading comprehension, translation, and vocabulary skills. Moreover, data indicated that in the case of the Chinese learner, discussion of previously unknown vocabulary included in the game text enhanced knowledge of aspects of the TL culture. Significant limitations of this study include its brief duration and anecdotal nature. Although as was observed above, the researchers claimed that reciprocal learning occurred, they provided no empirical evidence to substantiate this claim.

The Use of Text-Based Adventure Games in CALL

In early research, G. Jones (1986) reported on two experiments involving use of the text-based adventure game *Yellow River Kingdom*. As was stated in chapter 2, in this game each player adopts the role of the ruler of an imaginary country who must take decisions regarding the allocation of scarce resources in order to maintain the population. In the first experiment, an intermediate-level group of EFL students played the game and their oral TL output was recorded. The researcher anticipated that playing the game would elicit a wide range of TL production relating to game tasks including comparisons, speculations, the use of modals, and conditionals. Data analysis confirmed that playing the game elicited a great deal of TL output. However, this was limited in scope and restricted to the present tense. The most frequent types of utterance identified in the data were suggestions, agreements, and disagreements. Reactions to on-screen feedback included phatic utterances and interjections. The learner output was characterized by the use of a simple register that was appropriate to the context. Data showed that learner errors occurred frequently. In the second experiment, another learner group used the game in combination with an adversarial role-play where different dyads competed for scarce resources. The learners undertook an orientation that provided an overview of the game, and anticipated items were pre-taught. As was the case in the first experiment the interaction was video-recorded. The researcher anticipated that this approach would result in a much richer and differentiated range of expressions than that produced by the previous group. In a finding that was not anticipated, the learners rarely used the formal language taught in the orientation, but instead used an informal register that was appropriate to the peer-based nature of the interaction. Moreover, observation revealed that errors were less frequent and that the participants actively collaborated in order to achieve the best outcome against the game. Jones claimed that the game elicited high levels of learner motivation by providing an element of competition, and that the new data provided a stimulus that facilitated the production, and maintenance, of TL output. A further beneficial aspect of the game was the element of make-believe that engendered active participation. Although the limitations of the game were acknowledged, the researcher claimed that the game possessed potential as a learning tool. The researcher speculated that when carefully integrated into a wider teacher-managed activity the game had potential as a source of speaking practice for intermediate EFL learners.

Culley, Mulford, and Milbury-Steen (1986) used the French version of *Mystery House* as the basis for an experiment designed to explore the potential of this type of text-based adventure game as a means to elicit TL use. Six teachers and students of French and Latin were requested to imagine playing the game. After an orientation, when a game script and plot outline were provided, teachers adopted the role of the game and communicated using predesigned messages in real time with the students over a mainframe network. Data showed that the learners, who were novice players, experienced immediate difficulties due to their unfamiliarity with adventure game conventions. The researchers observed that the lack of any prior training and knowledge of the game's plot led the learners to respond inappropriately to prompts as they failed to grasp the mimetic conventions that govern adventure games. Moreover, although the learners had access to the game they failed to explore the virtual world and experienced high degrees of frustration, as they were unable to progress. Although the language used was limited in scope and contained errors it nonetheless contained a high degree of richness. Contrary to the expectation of the researchers the learners produced lengthy TL utterances. For the Latin learners these contained purposes clauses, ablative absolute constructions, and phrases that were not strictly necessary. In French, the learners used justificatory clauses and elaborate indirect discourse. In a significant finding, the researchers speculated that the lengthy TL output was the result of participants being aware that their teachers were present. Unfortunately the researchers did not conduct follow-up studies to explore this insight.

Exploratory research undertaken by Palmberg (1988) examined the use by two Swedish language learners of the adventure game *Pirate Cove*. This study was designed to investigate the potential of this type of game as a vocabulary learning tool for elementary English language learners. As was observed in chapter 2, the goal of the player in this game is to find a treasure chest hidden on one of ten islands shown on a map. Players navigate the world and manipulate virtual objects by typing commands. The game incorporates a limited range of English vocabulary items amounting to 118 different words. The study was undertaken in three stages. In the first stage, the learners who were native speakers of Swedish played the game for 45 minutes. The researcher was present and acted as an interpreter providing Swedish translations of unknown vocabulary. The second stage took place a month later. In the period prior to this session the learners had no access to the game. The learners played the game for the same amount of time as before and were asked to translate into Swedish any words displayed by the program. The third stage took place one month after the second session. As was the case in the second session, the learners had no prior access to the game. The learners were given a list of 50 English words that appeared in the game and were requested to provide Swedish translations. Researcher observation confirmed that the participants quickly mastered the game and could provide Swedish translations of the majority of vocabulary items that were encountered. The data from the second stage indicated that the learners appeared to have forgotten the meanings of approximately half the target vocabulary. Of the words they could recall the majority shared similarities with Swedish. However, the data from the third stage showed that participants could provide accurate translations of the meanings of 35 of the 50 target language words. Taken as whole, the findings indicate that the learners displayed a good receptive knowledge of a sample of vocabulary used in the game. Palmberg suggested that this finding provides evidence to support the contention that playing this game meets the language learning needs of young elementary learners by promoting vocabulary learning. However, this claim should be treated with a degree of caution, as only two learners participated in the study, making the findings difficult to generalize.

Cheung and Harrison (1992) investigated the use of *Colossal Adventure* with 84 university EFL students based in Hong Kong. This mixed-methods study was designed to explore the potential of participation in text-based adventure games as a means to improve knowledge and use of game-specific TL structures focusing on prepositions of place, lexical items, and conditionals. The study incorporated two stages with the learners divided into two groups. In the first stage, one group who were novices undertook a pre-study orientation session. They then played the game for eight hours over a two-week period. A second control group practiced word processing for four hours over the same period. On the conclusion of the above activities, both groups took an attainment text designed to establish if there were any gains in the above TL structures. In order to obtain data on attitudes a questionnaire was administered. In the second stage, the roles of the learner groups were switched with the control group engaging in eight hours of game play while the other group undertook four hours of word processing training. On completion of these activities the same attainment test and attitude questionnaire were administered. Quantitative data analysis established that in the first stage, there was no significant difference in learner performance between both groups with regard to knowledge of prepositions and conditionals. However, the performance of novice group was significantly higher in terms of program-specific lexical items. This finding appeared to be the result of this group having played the game. Data for the second stage showed significantly improved performance in the three areas that were the focus of investigation. The most significant improvements involved gains in program-specific lexical items. The researchers concluded that based on their results playing the game enabled the learners to improve their knowledge of program-specific lexical items. Feedback to the questionnaire indicated that the participants found the game challenging and that access to game-specific information would be helpful. In more positive findings, the majority of participants claimed that playing the game was an interesting and enjoyable experience. Most learners indicating that playing the game was a worthwhile activity and a useful means to practice English.

Early Research on Computer Games in CALL: Significant Findings

The analysis in this chapter draws attention to a number of limitations of early research on the use of text-manipulation and adventure games in CALL. These reflect many of the problems with CALL research identified in chapter 1. The majority of projects were of limited duration, and as the discussion shows, there were few longitudinal studies. Moreover, with the exception of the research project carried out by Cheung and Harrison (1992), the number of participants was small. The absence of control groups is a noteworthy feature of the majority of studies. Further problematic features of the research include a heavy reliance on learner self-reporting, and a general failure to recognize the potential influence of novelty effects. These factors coupled to the limited nature of the empirical work, make the findings problematic to generalize. In addition, the studies examined in this chapter were undertaken by individual or small groups of researchers, and did not form part of a systematic long-term research program. Another important issue raised in any examination of early work is that with the exception of the research undertaken by Legenhausen and Wolff (1990), the studies were not informed by explicit theories of SLA. The general absence of a theory-led approach represents an important finding that requires acknowledgment. However, this situation may, in part, reflect the experimental nature of the majority of the studies, and the limited extent of SLA research at the time. Although this body of research is subject to limitations it also provides potentially significant findings.

As table 5.1 shows, the majority of studies indicate that use of both text-manipulation and adventure games elicit the production and use of spoken and written TL output (Cheung and Harrison 1992, Culley, Mulford, and Milbury-Steen 1986, Johns and Wang 1999, G. Jones 1986, Legenhausen and Wolff 1990, Piper 1986). Research suggests that this phenomenon may be facilitated when the game is integrated into other related classroom activities (G. Jones 1986). Although this represents a positive finding, concerns were raised in the contemporary literature regarding the quality of the TL output. In a discussion of the findings reported by Piper (1986) on the use of a text-manipulation game Philips observes that

> thus when considering the linguistic value of games model programs, it is possible to distinguish between the real use of the language required to operate the game and the realistic use modeled in some form by the game. Much has been claimed for the value of the language generated in interaction among the students as they tackle programs of this type, not least by myself (Phillips, op. cit.). But it could well be that what is stimulated is only a highly restricted register relating to the language of operating games and solving problems. (Philips 1987, 279)

Piper identified this potential drawback of the computer games of the time and noted the repetitive nature of much of the TL produced by the learners in her study. Moreover, G. Jones (1986) reported that the TL output elicited by participation in a text-based adventure game was restricted to the present tense. In a related finding, although Legenhausen and Wolff (1990) stressed the benefits of a text-manipulation game in terms of opportunities to activate both explicit and partly implicit linguistic knowledge, they expressed

Table 5.1 Significant findings on the use of text-manipulation and adventure games in CALL

Positive findings	Negative findings
Active engagement	Production of a limited register
Production of TL output	Frequent production of errors
Limited evidence of vocabulary learning	Absence of a focus on form during gameplay
Positive learner feedback	Exposure to low frequency game-specific vocabulary
High degree of motivation	TL production isolated from a context for communication
	Need for training
	Few studies based on SLA theory

concerns regarding how SLA would be facilitated in the absence of a context for communication:

> The question, however, remains whether the activation of this knowledge contributes to their language learning in that it improves their productive and receptive L-2 competence. We rather tend to conclude that the activation of isolated bits of language knowledge detached from the overall context of language production or comprehension does not substantially further the learner's productive and receptive abilities. Whether the activation of linguistic knowledge (implicit or explicit) and the assumed transformation of implicit into explicit knowledge can be called language learning in any significant way is actually open to interpretation, and depends largely on one's language learning theory. We tend to believe that a foreign language is learnt more effectively when it is used in a more purposeful way. (Legenhausen and Wolff 1990, 7)

As may be observed in table 5.1, analysis of the findings on vocabulary learning presents a mixed picture. In her study on the conversational spin-off generated by use of text-manipulation games, Piper (1986, 196) showed that the vocabulary used by the learners was limited in scope, consisting primarily of brief utterances involving use of imperatives, expressions of agreement, and disagreement. In addition, Piper (1986) found that learners produced frequent errors. Higgins, Lawrie, and White (1999) reported a similar finding. Piper (1986) found no evidence of any focus on form as instances of self-correction were absent from her data. In contrast, Johns and Wang

(1999) claimed that the learners in their study gained valuable exposure to challenging TL vocabulary incorporated into a text-manipulation game. Findings on the use of text-based adventure games are also varied. G. Jones (1986) and Culley, Mulford, and Milbury-Steen (1986) identified a high incidence of learner errors. However, these researchers also reported the production of lengthy and lexically rich sentences. Contemporary researchers most notably C. Jones (1986) further emphasized that the fantasy theme common to these games presents exposure to low frequency vocabulary that is of limited relevance to the needs of learners. In contrast, other studies have reported evidence for vocabulary learning. As the discussion of the findings reported by Palmberg (1988) shows learners displayed good recall of game-related vocabulary. Moreover, the findings of the large-scale study conducted by Cheung and Harrison (1992) provided credible, though not conclusive, empirical evidence that playing an adventure game elicited retention of game-specific lexical items.

A further issue identified in early research is the need for learner training. This factor appears particularly significant in relation to text-based adventure games where learners must familiarize themselves with game objectives, story lines, and more complex interfaces (G. Jones 1986). In their innovative research, Culley, Mulford, and Milbury-Steen (1986) reported that learners who lacked familiarity with the conventions unique to this specific game genre experienced considerable difficulties in progressing in the game, and this situation led to frustration. A similar finding was echoed in the learner feedback reported by Cheung and Harrison (1992). These researchers observed that the learners in their study claimed that the challenging nature of the game required that information relating to game background and objectives be provided prior to gaming sessions. The learners commented that gameplay would be facilitated if learning support features such as dictionaries were available.

CALL researchers have long emphasized the beneficial effects of the high degree of motivation that is frequently engendered by computer games (Higgins and Johns 1984). The findings examined in this discussion draw attention to this phenomenon with regard to both text-manipulation and adventure games. The learners in the study conducted by Higgins, Lawrie, and White (1999) appeared highly engaged by game activities. Similar findings are evident in the data provided by Johns and Wang (1999), Legenhausen and Wolff (1990), and Piper (1986). As has been observed at an earlier stage of this discussion, G. Jones (1986) claimed that the element of competition inherent to adventure games supported high levels of motivation and engagement, particularly when the game is combined with a conventional classroom activity. Cheung and Harrison (1992) highlight generally favorable learner attitudes, with the majority of participants in their study claiming that although the game was challenging, it was interesting, and enjoyable to play. In a further noteworthy finding, these researchers observed that learners were willing to spend considerable amounts of time on the game.

This discussion shows that early studies on the use of text-manipulation and adventure games in CALL are subject to a number of limitations. However, this early body of work is nonetheless valuable, as it identifies a number of potential benefits of playing computer games. As the following chapter will show, although text-manipulation and adventure games remain in use, contemporary research has largely been concerned with investigating newer computer games. The discussion in the next chapter will show that although technological developments, most notably the emergence of powerful low-cost computers and the rise of the Internet, have continued to play a central role in development work on the use of computer games in CALL, SLA research has had a greater influence than was the case in the past. The following chapter examines more recent work on the use of computer games in CALL.

CHAPTER 6

Recent Studies on Computer Gaming in CALL: An Analysis of Findings

Computer Games in Language Education: Recent Studies

Research on the use of computer games in CALL has expanded in recent years due, in part, to developments in computing and communication technologies. The widespread availability of powerful low-cost personal computers with advanced graphics capabilities, accessible game consoles, and mobile communication devices such as smart phones, has stimulated the development of new types of games. Modern computer games offer access to challenging and highly engaging player experiences that were not possible in the past due to technological limitations. The spread of the Internet has facilitated the emergence of online gaming as a pervasive worldwide phenomenon (Gee 2007b). Moreover, the development of SLA theory has also influenced recent research work on many aspects of CALL, including the use of computer games (Thorne, Black, and Sykes 2009). CALL researchers have explored the use of both commercial and educational games that are designed specifically to facilitate learning (Peterson 2010). As this research has yet to be the subject of comprehensive investigation, this chapter will analyze the findings of studies that involve the game types described in chapter 2. Following the procedures described in the previous chapter, studies conducted over the past ten years are selected from the available literature. Seventeen studies that focus specifically on learner gameplay are subject to detailed analysis. The following discussion focuses on specific areas, such as, for example, assumptions, design, methods of data collection, use of statistics, and appropriateness of conclusions.

Research on Simulation Games

CALL researchers have explored use of 2D and 3D-based simulation games in a number of studies. Coleman (2002) reported on research involving beginning-level ESL writing students that utilized the freeware element of the flight simulation game *Sim Copter* that is based on the commercial game *The Sims*. As was observed in chapter 2, in this game, the player assumes the role of a helicopter pilot who must navigate around a virtual city rendered in 2D graphics in order to complete a number of program generated tasks. In this semester-long study that formed part of a prefreshman composition course, the learners were required to undertake specific tasks designed to raise awareness of the concept of writing for an audience. During an orientation briefing the learners were provided with an overview of the simulation, and received web-based instructions on the specific keyboard commands required to fly the helicopter, and walk around the city. In the execution phase, the participants worked in small groups on the following tasks. In the first task, they adopted the role of the helicopter pilot or copilot who must locate a specific location in the simulation and then write directions for a VIP visitor on how to walk there at a later time. In the second task, they assume the identity of a VIP visitor who must use another participant's directions in order to visit a specific location within the simulation. Based on learner feedback obtained during the post-study debriefing, Coleman claimed the project configuration that combined use of a realistic simulation for role-plays with drafting of directions in order to complete authentic problem-based tasks offered a number of benefits. Observation revealed that the game elicited a high degree of collaboration as learners actively assisted each other in drafting directions and during the role-play. This situation resulted in the consistent production of coherent and purposeful TL output. The researcher further asserted that although the learners encountered difficulties, the ability to leave the simulation and reenter in a different role was valuable, as it appeared to raise learner awareness of writing for an audience by creating a realistic environment that is not possible with pen and paper simulations. Although this innovative research produced encouraging findings, it is subject to a significant limitation: namely, the number of participants was not specified, making the findings difficult to generalize.

Miller and Hegelheimer (2006) conducted a mixed-methods research project on learner use of the 3D simulation game *The Sims*. This game simulates the challenges of real life and presents a realistic and complex scenario whereby players must organize and manage an American neighborhood of ten houses. Players create characters that engage in tasks relevant to everyday life such as shopping and working. They are further required to satisfy character needs and react to events that occur in the game. The above researchers note that although this game is very popular it was designed to meet the needs of native speakers based in the United States. As a result of this situation, they explored the use of the game in combination with supporting materials designed to enhance vocabulary learning. A total of 18 intermediate-level EFL learners based at a university in the United States took part in this research that formed part of a semester-long academic literacy class. Although the number of participants in this study was limited, the researchers adopted a counterbalance research design in order to maximize data collection, reduce the variability of experimental errors, and analyze treatment effects. The participants were assigned to six groups of three students each based on responses to a pre-project survey and pretest. Each group was assigned to a computer station that contained one computer to play the game. Another computer provided instructions and supplementary materials. After participating in a tutorial the groups experienced each of the following conditions. In the first condition, learners played the game and were required to access structured supplementary materials consisting of lists of vocabulary that appeared in the game, an online dictionary, descriptions of significant grammar features, grammar quizzes based on phrases taken from the game, and explanatory culture notes. In the second condition, access to the above materials was optional while in the third condition no supplementary materials were provided. Learner data was collected from weekly quizzes, post-study surveys, and questionnaires.

The data was subjected to quantitative and qualitative analysis. Quantitative analysis of postgame quiz scores was conducted using a t-test followed by a Tukey-Kramer post hoc test. Results revealed statistically significant differences. In terms of vocabulary acquisition, the learners who experienced the first condition outperformed those who experienced the other conditions. Participant feedback was subject to qualitative analysis, and this showed statistically significant differences indicating that the supplementary materials were viewed as helpful, and that of these materials, the vocabulary activity was perceived as the most valuable. Moreover, the majority of participants claimed that the supplementary materials facilitated the successful completion of game tasks. The researchers claimed that a beneficial aspect of the game is the focus it provides on specific linguistic features. The results are important, as this well-designed study provides credible empirical evidence to support the researchers' assertion that when simulation games are combined with carefully designed supplementary materials that draw on lexis used in the game, and that provide explicit instruction, the acquisition of vocabulary may be enhanced.

In another study on the use of *The Sims* with intermediate-level ESL learners, Ranalli (2008) attempted to build on the work of Miller and Hegelheimer (2006) by employing mixed methods to examine learner attitudes and the influence of specially designed supplementary materials on vocabulary knowledge. In this research, the design and supplementary materials were similar to those used by Miller and Hegelheimer (2006). However, this research differed in a number of respects. The study was explicitly motivated by cognitive SLA research on vocabulary learning. Moreover, the number of participants was smaller. The participants worked in dyads, and in order to achieve counterbalancing these were rotated randomly so that each dyad experienced all three experimental conditions. Pre- and posttests along with weekly quizzes were used to investigate vocabulary learning. Participant attitudes were explored by means of pre- and post-study surveys. In a finding that mirrors results reported by Miller and Hegelheimer (2006), quantitative analysis of test and quiz scores established that combining gameplay with access to supplementary materials contributed to statistically significant improvements in knowledge of vocabulary that appeared in the game. Responses to the post-study survey indicated generally favorable attitudes toward use of supplementary materials when playing the game. Participants claimed that playing with a partner was enjoyable and that dyad members assisted each other in understanding unfamiliar words and phrases. Learner feedback expressed a range of attitudes toward the game's potential as a language-learning tool. A majority of learners agreed that they learned new words and expressions. However, some learners claimed that the game could be difficult to play and identified the lack of guidance and spoken English as issues. Ranalli acknowledged the limitations of this study, namely, the small sample size, and the risks associated with self-reporting. Nevertheless, he claimed that his findings establish that when commercial simulation games are combined with carefully designed supplementary materials, ESL students from diverse backgrounds can play them successfully in order to facilitate improvements in vocabulary knowledge. Significant features of this study include its grounding in cognitive SLA research, use of counterbalancing, and analysis of a variety of data sources. This study is also noteworthy as it represents one of the few attempts in the literature to build on prior work on a specific aspect of learning involving a particular game type in a systematic manner.

Anderson et al. (2008) carried out experimental work that examined use of the military simulation game *America's Army*. This mixed-methods research explored feasibility, learner attitudes, and possible effects on listening comprehension of exposure to in-game TL dialogue. The research involved two stages. In the first stage, eight EFL learners worked in small groups and undertook five game sessions in which a teacher guided them through training modules. In order to establish the feasibility of using the game as a tool in CALL, researcher observation was conducted. Learner attitudes were investigated in post-study interviews held after the game sessions. Learner feedback indicated that playing the game was perceived by the learners as a means to improve their English. Learners asserted that the provision of a glossary would facilitate learning. In their comments they suggested that headphones were required in order to enable a focus on the spoken dialogues. The second stage investigated the possible influence of gameplay on listening comprehension and learner attitudes. Before gameplay, 17 male and 12 female Taiwanese engineering majors were randomly assigned to one of two conditions. One group received instruction covering ten words that occurred repeatedly in the game. The other group received instruction on how to navigate through the game. A ten-minute web-based listening comprehension pretest was administered. Then the participants were randomly assigned into groups that received instruction in either vocabulary or game navigation. On completion of this activity, the learners worked together for 30 minutes to complete the initial training module. Two teachers were present and provided assistance. The learners were allowed to repeat this activity for additional practice. They then undertook another module for ten minutes. After this activity, a web-based ten-minute listening comprehension posttest and questionnaire were administered. Learner activity was observed and video-recorded.

Statistical analysis of the pre- and post-study listening test scores found no significant differences between the two groups. Questionnaire data revealed that the learners had a positive attitude toward using the game as a learning tool. Moreover, learners expressed the view that the support of the instructor was necessary during gameplay. The majority of participants, who rated their level of English proficiency as low, found the conversation difficult to follow, and claimed that they were unfamiliar with military terminology. The learners encountered difficulties following instructions, interacting in the game, and in the training module. There were significant differences in gender attitudes toward playing the game. The male subjects claimed the game was fun to play, while the female subjects expressed a general lack of interest in the subject matter. A noteworthy feature of this experimental study was the use of mixed methods in order to investigate listening comprehension and learner attitudes. However, this work is also subject to limitations including its relatively brief duration, and the somewhat superficial investigation of learner attitudes.

Research on Role-Playing Games

MMORPGs have been a major focus of recent research on the use of computer games in CALL. Rankin, Gold, and Gooch (2006) reported on a pilot project that utilized *Ever Quest 2*. An initial training session was provided that involved an introduction to the game story line, instructions, combat, character classes, and vocabulary. Four ESL students who had limited experience of computer games then played the game for a minimum of four hours a week over a period of a month. The student's text chat was recorded and their gameplay observed. Feedback was obtained from periodic discussions with learners who also completed a post-study questionnaire, and were interviewed. In order to measure improvements in vocabulary, the researchers compared the learners understanding of specific vocabulary that was used at least once in the game and vocabulary that was used more than five times during learner interactions with non-player characters. Data showed that there were variations in learner performance and that these appeared linked to proficiency level. The researchers claimed that the intermediate and advanced-level learners increased their English vocabulary by 40 percent through interactions with nonplaying game characters. Analysis indicated that these learners displayed high levels of accuracy in defining the meanings of new vocabulary that appeared more than five times during in-game interactions. These learners increased their production of TL linguistic output by 100 percent over the duration of the research. The game appeared unsuitable for the beginner-level learner who was observed to experience cognitive overload. The majority of the learners expressed positive views on the use of the game as language learning tool. This group indicated that, although challenging, playing the game was beneficial in terms of vocabulary, reading comprehension, and conversational skills. One of the participants further claimed that *Ever Quest 2* was fun to play. Learners identified a number of areas where the game could be improved. For example, they indicated a preference for more feedback and suggested that audio should be included with non-player agents. They also indicated that language support features should be incorporated into the game. Although this pilot study reported positive findings, it is subject to a number of significant limitations. Only eight game sessions were held over a period of one month. The brief duration of the project and small number of participants represent limitations. Moreover, the design of this study did not draw on any explicit theory of SLA.

In a descriptive case study Thorne (2008) examined, from a sociocultural perspective, the in-game interaction of two players in the MMORPG *World of Warcraft*. One player was based in the United States the other in the Ukraine. Chat transcripts were collected, and this source of data was supplemented by researcher observation. An informal follow-up interview was conducted with the American participant. Analysis showed that playing the game engendered a high degree of motivation. Many of the constructs proposed in sociocultural accounts of SLA appeared in the data. Thorne reported evidence that the two players utilized English in order to actively engage in TL dialogue during in-game quests. The gamers undertook interaction where they assumed the roles of expert and novice. This context for interaction facilitated reciprocity, negotiation of game activities, requests for assistance, repair sequences, experimentation, and explicit corrective feedback. The supportive nature of the interaction was reflected in the collaborative social relationship established by the gamers, who utilized politeness and humor in order maintain the affiliative bond that had developed during their gameplay. Thorne claimed that the game provided a context that is beneficial for language socialization and learning. He further asserted that the setting provided by MMORPGs and other informal learning environments made possible by the rapid expansion of the Internet should be included selectively in contemporary L2 pedagogy. A positive feature of this study was its firm grounding in SLA research. However, this descriptive research involved only two participants, and the Ukrainian learner was not interviewed, leaving the important issue of learner attitudes unexplored.

A large-scale study undertaken by Suh, S. Kim, and N. Kim (2010) reported on the effectiveness of an educational MMORPG compared to conventional modes of instruction. The participants were 220 EFL students based at an elementary school in South Korea. The learners in this two-month project were divided into two groups. The learners in the experimental group took a test of basic language skills and were divided into subgroups based on their scores. These groups undertook two 40-minute game sessions per week in the English language MMORPG *Nori School*. This game is purpose-built for language education, incorporating avatars, and text chat. Players can undertake individual and team-based gameplay with the objective of saving a village. In an attempt to achieve this goal, players must try to obtain items that make game activities easier and facilitate progression to higher levels in the game. In-game tasks include fighting monsters, trading items, and completing quizzes that focus on reading, listening, and writing. Players can watch animations, read stories, and participate in a guild system that is designed to facilitate collaboration and joint problem solving. The control group undertook conventional textbook-based language instruction covering content similar to that in the game supported by multimedia courseware. The researchers used quantitative and qualitative methods including pre- and posttests, and a survey, in order to establish the most effective method of instruction in terms of learning achievement. Statistical analysis was employed to determine the influence of the following variables on achievement; gender, prior knowledge, motivation, self-directed learning, computer skills, game skills, network capacity, and computer accessibility. The analysis showed that there were no significant differences between the two groups in learning achievement. However, it was found that the learners who played the game made more gains in reading, writing, and listening. The data indicated that of the variables investigated only prior knowledge, motivation, and network speed influenced achievement. Prior knowledge made the most significant contribution to English achievement followed by motivation and network speed. The researchers claimed that the game may be a useful means to develop English skills and that optimizing the environment to prevent network issues is crucial in supporting learner motivation and performance.

The findings of this study are significant for the following reasons. This research involved a large number of participants and investigated learner performance over a longer period than many other studies. A mixed-methods approach was used that combined rigorous empirical data analysis tools such as t-tests and ANOVA with a survey in order to provide a board perspective on the data. A further significant feature of this study was its comparative nature. Moreover, as this discussion shows, to date, few large-scale studies have employed control groups, or have attempted to compare gameplay to other forms of learning. This research was not informed by a specific theory of language learning and this represents a limitation. However, this study is nonetheless important, as it is one of the few attempts reported in the literature to explore the influence of a range of variables on learner achievement.

Reinders and Wattana (2011) investigated EFL learner's gameplay in and attitudes toward a modified version of the commercial MMORPG *Ragnarok Online*. The story line in this game draws on Norse mythology and a popular Korean comic book. The participants were 16 IT students from a university in Thailand who possessed beginner and intermediate levels of English language proficiency. The study was designed to explore the quantity and quality of the second language interaction engendered by playing the game and possible effects on willingness to communicate. Of the three 40-minute quests that were undertaken only text and voice chat transcript data from the first and third quests was analyzed. This data was supplemented by questionnaires administered after each session. These were designed to investigate the effects of the game on willingness to communicate. The learners were provided with an orientation and participated in a collaborative debriefing after each session. They accessed a modified version of *Ragnarok Online* run on a private server and played the game in a university computer lab. The modified quests presented authentic scenarios requiring purposeful interaction in TL and formed part of a regular language course. The quests were based on content drawn from this course and were appropriate to the learner's language level. The gameplay involved user controlled characters undertaking quests such as, for example, combat with monsters and quizzes, in order to gain rewards and experiences necessary for progression to higher levels. The quests required text and voice-based interaction with other players and non-player characters.

The researchers found that playing the game had positive effects on the quantity of TL output produced by the participants. Quantitative analysis of the voice and text chat data confirmed that in both mediums the learners produced more and longer turns between the sessions. In addition, analysis revealed that in both types of chat the amount of TL output in terms of words and turns increased between sessions one and three. However, the quality of the second language interaction was variable. The data suggested that although playing the game elicited the production of a wide variety of discourse functions, in terms of accuracy and complexity the quality of participants TL output did not improve. The researchers suggested this finding may be due to the cognitive demands of the communication environment provided by the game. There were also differences in the type of TL output produced by each medium. Politeness involving greetings was more frequent in the oral chat. Moreover, clarification requests were frequent in both oral and written chat. However, they were more frequent in the former mode of communication. The need to proceed in the game resulted in the production of a large number of confirmation checks during oral chat. This type of TL output was not found in the text chat data. Moreover, self-correction and various types of question were more frequent in the written chat. The researchers speculated that this finding was the product of the extra time provided. Grammatical and lexical accuracy was found to be higher in the text chat. The voice chat contained instances of first language (henceforth L1) vocabulary. The researchers observed that the absence of many paralinguistic cues and time pressures resulted in the production of a simplified register that contained emoticons, misspellings, article omissions, contractions, and abbreviations. In their questionnaire feedback, the learners expressed broadly positive views, and statistical analysis of responses confirmed that willingness to communicate was enhanced. The majority of participants identified beneficial aspects of playing the game including improved comprehension, exposure to new vocabulary, enjoyment, and fluency practice. However, a minority who reported poor communication skills and low confidence levels found the game challenging. This group did not achieve any improvement.

Although learner data was only collected from two game sessions, and the number of participants was limited, the findings are noteworthy. This research provides empirical evidence confirming that gameplay in a MMORPG when combined with modified quests that are based on learner needs, and that draw on content from a regular language course, elicits statistically significant increases in TL output over time. Another significant finding was the differences in the quality of the TL produced during text and voice chat-based TL interaction within the game. The findings on learner feedback provide evidence suggesting that participation in MMORPG-based gaming enhances learner willingness to communicate.

Piirainen-Marsh and Tainio (2009) carried out qualitative research on the use by EFL learners of the console-based role-playing game *Final Fantasy X* in an informal setting. The two male subjects in this study were adolescent native speakers of Finnish who had prior experience of playing the above game. The researchers recorded five hours of participant gameplay. In this game, player progress is determined by dialogue among the central avatar-based characters. The game is set in a fictional world and provides plot driven narrative episodes where players are required to undertake various quests in order to defeat an evil force. The research design was strongly influenced by sociocultural SLA research that views TL interaction and repetition as playing important roles in language development. The researchers utilized conversation analysis to examine repetition of game character's utterances elicited during play. Their analysis established that the use of repetition enabled the learners to collaborate, and develop their TL competence through interaction involving co-construction, experimentation, and socialization. The data indicated that prosodic and lexical repetitions were used repeatedly in four distinct cases. In the first case, a player repeated an utterance adjacent to the source turn. In the second case, a player reproduced a previous utterance in anticipation of its use. In the third case, a player recontextualized a prior utterance in order to use it in a new setting. In the final case, a player expanded creatively on utterances made previously and repeated by one of the players. The researchers claimed that the repetition elicited by unfolding events in the game served as a resource for participation while performing the important functions of signaling attention and interest. This phenomenon also facilitated social interaction, enjoyment, collaborative play, and membership of the player community. They further asserted that the data showed how repetition produced a context conducive to learning by focusing learner attention on specific aspects of TL use. This study is valuable in that it represents one of the few attempts to utilize conversation analysis in order to investigate, at a micro level, the interactional and social practices elicited by a role-playing game. The presence in the data of constructs identified in sociocultural SLA theory is significant and draws attention to the need for further research on learner interaction, socialization, play, and repetition engendered by this type of game in informal out-of-school contexts.

Research on Multiuser Virtual Environments (MUVEs)

As was observed in chapter 2, MUVEs have been created that incorporate games designed to facilitate language learning. In preliminary research, Johnson (2007) investigated the use of an early version of *The Tactical Language and Culture Training System* (TLCTS) in the teaching of Arabic. This system utilizes AI and speech recognition technologies to process learner speech during lessons incorporating exercises and quizzes that require TL production and understanding. TLCTS presents access to glossaries, grammar explanations, and culture notes. A further element of the system is a modified version of a commercial game engine that is specifically designed for use by military personnel. This includes an arcade game where the players use spoken commands in order to move their avatar around a realistic 3D virtual world. A mission-based game is provided in which players are immersed in serious game scenarios modeled on real-world situations likely to be encountered in military operations. In the mission game, the player must utilize the TL so that their avatar can interact in real time with system generated non-player characters in order to accomplish specific tasks. The game content draws on the dialogue-based interactive lessons that are designed to facilitate the development of specific TL skills involved in communication and cultural understanding. An evaluation of the Iraqi Arabic version of TLCTS known as *Tactical Iraqi*, was conducted after the system had undergone an initial series of pilots that involved using the system in training courses with Marine Corps personnel. The participants were 20 Marines who had, with one exception, no previous knowledge of Arabic. Nine of the participants had undertaken a tour of duty in Iraq. Learner attitudes were mixed and appeared influenced by prior expectations and experiences. Of the participants who had been to Iraq, 78 percent claimed that they had acquired functional Arabic after using the system for 50 hours. This group gave the system a grading of four on a one-to-five scale and provided useful feedback on improvements. Participants who had not been to Iraq were less enthusiastic with only 22 percent claiming any functional ability. Moreover, these learners gave the system a lower grading. Johnson speculated that one possible reason for the discrepancy in findings lies in the fact that the version used was designed for the Army rather than the Marines. The feedback reported in this pilot study suggests that negative learner attitudes may be elicited when game content does not meet learner expectations. However, the findings should be treated with a degree of caution, as the number of participants was limited. Furthermore, no detail was provided on the data collection tools used to elicit learner feedback.

Zheng et al. (2009) undertook a qualitative case study that analyzed, from a sociocultural SLA perspective, the interaction of EFL learners in the MUVE *Quest Atlantis*. This educational environment is designed for children and provides access to a high quality digitally rendered 3D theme-based virtual world that incorporates gaming. Players are provided with real-time communication tools, quests, a point reward system, and personal avatars. The researchers examined the after-school gameplay of two non-native speakers of English based in China. These learners formed dyads with two native speakers located in the United States in order to undertake three 90-minute co-quests that were completed during a larger study conducted over ten weeks. This study utilized iterative multilayered analysis. The researchers employed discourse analysis of transcripts, observation, and interviews. Analysis revealed the presence of constructs hypothesized in sociocultural accounts of SLA. During the quests the learners and their partners actively collaborated and engaged in social interaction. They undertook purposeful, meaning-focused co-construction in the TL. In completing the quests, the learners utilized repair moves involved in the negotiation of meaning. These included use of clarification requests, comprehension, and confirmation checks. In an interesting finding, it was found that during scaffolding the participants engaged in reciprocal action involving feedback, and rotated the roles of instructor and learner depending on the nature of the quest. There was evidence that the learners used utterances designed to signal interest and engaged in self- and other-initiated correction. The learners not only negotiated content at the utterance level, they actively expressed their cultural identities, thus raising their partners' intercultural awareness. In their feedback, the learners commented favorably on the opportunities provided for TL practice and use. The researchers claimed that the goal-directed and authentic context elicited collaboration involving TL use, providing resources for emergent identity formation, meaning making, socialization, and SLA.

The findings of this study are important for a number of reasons. This research represents one of the few attempts to utilize a case study to investigate learner interaction during gameplay in a MUVE. The use of a case study that incorporated a range of data sources supported the identification of significant patterns and themes in the data, and offered the additional advantage of facilitating triangulation. These aspects of the research lend credibility to the findings. Moreover, this study confirms the presence of constructs identified in sociocultural SLA. The detailed nature of the analysis facilitated the identification of significant findings at both a macro and micro level. Moreover, the use of discourse analysis provides a window on the language development of individual participants.

An exploratory case study undertaken by Liang (2011) focused on *Erie Isle*, a role-playing game located in the popular MUVE *Second Life*. The learners in this research were 11 undergraduates of upper intermediate-level of English proficiency drawn from two elective classes. Seven of the volunteer participants were novice users of *Second Life*. The learners were provided with training, and in addition, undertook a two-hour preparation session where they rehearsed the roles and personalities they would adopt during their role-plays in the game. They then formed two teams and played the game for two hours. Data was collected from observation, written reports, chat transcripts, and video recordings. These data sources were supplemented by informal interviews with the participants. Analysis indicated that the game elicited a high degree of participation, collaboration, and the production of TL dialogue incorporating language play. Pragmatic play was the most frequent accounting for 47.5 percent of turns involving language play. This was followed by form-based play 20.1 percent, and semantic play 18.2 percent. A total of 14.2 percent of turns involved the mixing of two or more forms of play. Individual amounts and rates of play varied widely, reflecting learner differences in proficiency levels and learning styles. For example, a learner of high proficiency played primarily with linguistic forms. In contrast, five of the participants drew on their L1 to perform semantic and pragmatic play. The play was characterized by the use of humor, parody, mimicry, metaphor, and code switching. During the gameplay, the learners negotiated meanings and provided scaffolding. Although errors appeared in the data, the consistent production of complex TL led Liang to claim that role-playing games when combined with appropriate contextual support, have the potential to be used as an effective pedagogical tool. The researcher acknowledged a limitation of this research, namely, the small sample size.

Research on a First Person Shooter Game

Stubbs (2003) conducted a pilot project on the first person shooter game *Kana No Senshi*. This game is an adaption of the typing tutor program *The Typing of the Dead*. As was noted in chapter 2, this game is designed to facilitate the study of Japanese kana characters. Players must kill approaching zombies within a certain time frame by typing the correct romanization of kana characters that are displayed next to each zombie. The game incorporates a scoring system and provides real-time feedback on learner progress.

Six beginner-level students of Japanese played the game and then used a conventional kana learning program. The researcher observed the learners and administered a postgame survey. The findings indicated there were no significant differences in student performance between the two platforms. Stubbs claimed that the participants were observed to type more quickly when using the game. Learner feedback was positive with all of the learners stating that playing the game was more fun than the conventional program. Based on this finding, Stubbs claimed that the game was at least as effective as a traditional interface and that it was more entertaining. This pilot study is subject to a number of limitations. No background information on the participants or the context was provided. The design features of the conventional program were not discussed. Moreover, the duration of the project was not specified. These limitations make the findings difficult to generalize.

Research on a 3D Adventure Game

As was noted in chapter 2, in a 3D adventure game the player takes on the role of a protagonist in an interactive story, and explores an online environment incorporating high-quality graphics. In order to progress through the game the player must overcome a number of challenges that involve solving puzzles. Chen and Yang (2011) reported on learner attitudes toward the commercial 3D adventure game *Bone*. A group of 35 intermediate-level EFL students based at a university in Taiwan undertook a training session, and then played the game as a homework. On completing this activity, the learners wrote a short report on their experiences. They also completed a survey that contained ten five-scale and three open questions. Analysis of the feedback produced mixed findings. The learners identified a number of beneficial aspects of the design, including challenging missions, and an engaging story that encouraged them to continue playing. Participants commented favorably on the sense of achievement engendered by successfully completing difficult missions. A minority claimed the game was enjoyable to play and that it provided exposure to colloquial usages. Problematic aspects of the game design identified by the learners included lack of online help during the more challenging activities and a lack of time to complete certain missions. In a positive finding, the majority of learner responses indicated that playing the game helped to improve English skills. The learners identified listening, reading, and vocabulary skills as areas that were improved. In contrast, playing the game did not, in the learners view, improve speaking or writing skills. A minority commented that the speaking speed of the online characters encountered in the game was, on occasion, too fast to follow, and that the subtitles contained unfamiliar abbreviations that appeared too briefly. The students expressed a desire to be able to control aspects of the game such as dialogues and subtitles. Furthermore, no improvements in grammar knowledge were reported. The researchers acknowledged limitations of the research design. For example, only one game was investigated, and no pre- or posttests were administered in order to establish possible learning gains. However, the researchers did not discuss other limitations. For example, no observation of the participants' gameplay was undertaken. In addition, no post-study interviews were conducted.

Research on a Sports Game

Research on the use of the Japanese language sports game *Jiikyoo Pawafuru Yakkyu 6* was reported by deHaan (2005). As was noted in chapter 2, in this action-driven game the player is immersed in a simulated Japanese professional baseball game and assumes the role of player. The goal of this study was to establish if playing the game enhanced listening comprehension and kanji character recognition. An American undergraduate learner of Japanese as a foreign language took part in the research. Although an experienced computer gamer, this learner had not played the game prior to the study. A pretest of 55 kanji characters was administered. This involved the participant writing the pronunciations of characters he recognized. This was followed by a native speaker of Japanese reading 47 common words and expressions from the game while the learner was requested to translate their meanings orally. The learner was then required to play the game for one hour and ask questions to the researcher. As was the case with the pretest this activity was recorded. The learner then played the game for approximately an hour a week over a one-month period and was encouraged to complete a game log after each session. Seven of these were emailed to the researcher. After one month, the participant completed the same kanji test that was administered previously along with the same aural translation task. At this time, the learner played the game again for one hour, asked the researcher questions, and took part in an interview. These activities were recorded in a manner similar to the initial session. In comments to the researcher, the participant observed that it was difficult to balance gameplay with language learning. However, feedback indicated that the learner enjoyed playing the game and that it was interesting. The learner also claimed that his listening comprehension and game skills improved over time. The claim made regarding improved listening was confirmed in the second aural test when it was found that seven additional expressions were correctly translated. In the second interview, the learner claimed that his reading comprehension improved.

Data analysis confirmed this finding. On the second kanji test the learner was able to provide the pronunciation of 12 more kanji that had been the case previously. Moreover, during the second observation, the researcher noted that the learner was able to correctly pronounce the names of other players before they were announced. In feedback, the learner remarked that the ability to actively control aspects of the game such as using the pause feature was beneficial. The researcher speculated that repeated exposure to the limited number of TL utterances incorporated in the game coupled to the presentation of aural and written language provided a context conducive to learning.

The researcher noted several limitations of the research design utilized in this study including the small sample size, reliance on learner self-reporting, and the use of the same tests. However, the above study is subject to a number of other limitations that were not acknowledged by the researcher. One issue with the research design is the limited duration of the data collection period. Data was only collected over a relatively brief period. Another potential issue with this research is the appropriateness of the conclusions. For example, there was no discussion of the possible influence of participation in other courses. The possibility remains that the claimed improvement in listening skills was the result of the learners' participation in other Japanese language courses that occurred at the same time as this research. This suggests that the findings should be treated with some caution.

Research on a Rhythm Game

A large-scale mixed-methods study by deHaan, Reed, and Kuwada (2010) examined from the perspective of cognitive SLA theory how the interactivity provided by the rhythm game *Parappa the Rapper 2* described in chapter 2 influenced noticing and recall of English vocabulary. A total of 80 undergraduate Japanese EFL learners located at a university in Japan participated in this research. The learners had extensive experience of playing computer games. However, none of the participants had prior experience of playing the above game. The learners were assigned to dyads based on language and gaming proficiencies. Dyad members did not differ significantly in terms of their ages, gender, level of English proficiency, and self-reported pretreatment knowledge of vocabulary used in the game. After taking a vocabulary pretest, one learner in each dyad played the game for 20 minutes while the other watched the gameplay in real time on a monitor. Data was collected using a postgame vocabulary recall test, a cognitive load measure, and an experience questionnaire. In addition, a vocabulary recall test was administered two weeks after the experiment. Statistical analysis was conducted involving use of paired-samples t-tests and this revealed that learners from both groups recalled vocabulary from the game. Moreover, it was found that participants who played the game recalled significantly less vocabulary than the watchers. This result appeared to be the product of the extraneous cognitive load induced by the interactivity of the game. Feedback data indicated that the learners who played the game perceived it to be more difficult than the watchers did. Furthermore, the players claimed that playing the game while at the same time attending to its language was challenging. The data also showed that although the players enjoyed the game both groups forgot significant amounts of vocabulary. The researchers claimed based on their findings that, although the game provided access to comprehensible TL input, its complex nature caused many participants to experience cognitive overload. They concluded that before selecting a computer game for use in the classroom, educators should carefully consider the interactivity provided by different game genres and utilize pedagogically appropriate scaffolding.

The results of this research are important for a number of reasons. This study was firmly grounded in cognitive SLA research focusing on noticing and recall. Unlike the majority of the studies analyzed in this discussion, a large number of learners with similar L1 backgrounds and levels of gaming experience participated. The selection of learners with extensive gaming experience may have reduced the influence of novelty effects. This factor, coupled to the large sample size, represent beneficial aspects of the design that lend credibility to the results. Furthermore, the collection of multiple sources of data, and the use of a variety of quantitative data analysis instruments facilitated a comprehensive analysis and are further strengths of the design. The use of a delayed vocabulary recall test is particularly significant and lends credence to the findings, as the use of this data collection tool is infrequent in the literature.

Research on a Text-Based Adventure Game

A study undertaken by Neville, Shelton, and McInnis (2009) reported on learner vocabulary retention, transfer, and attitudes toward the game *Ausflug Nach Munchen*. The participants were undergraduate students of German as a foreign language on a course based at a university in the United States. This research involved two distinct learner groups and studies. The control group in the first study consisted of eight learners selected at random. This group was required to read a German short story of approximately 600 words and complete a homework activity based on vocabulary used in the text. The members of this group were also required to write a short essay. The second experimental group comprised seven students who played the game that covered the same scenario and contained the same vocabulary as the text studied by the control group. This group undertook the same homework assignment as the control group. The homework included matching, fill-in-the-blanks, word field, and essay composition elements. The homework contained a questionnaire made up of Likert scale questions designed to elicit feedback focusing on perceived task difficulty, mental effort on task, sense of immersion, enjoyment, and engagement. On the following day, learners in both groups completed an assessment that recorded vocabulary retention and transfer. The second study involved the same activities and data collection methods used in the first study. However, this study ran over three days and included an in-class debriefing on aspects of the game.

The data analysis highlights a number of interesting findings. Learner feedback on participating in the first project indicated that control group viewed the traditional methods they used to learn German vocabulary as superior. This group expressed higher confidence and satisfaction levels than the experimental group. However, data showed that the control group overestimated their actual performance as it was found the experimental group performed better on the homework and the assessment. Learner feedback highlighted a number of problems with the game. Although the researchers had incorporated help features, participants expressed frustration at their inability to make progress and at the challenging nature of the game. Learner feedback on the second study showed enhanced levels of comfort. The researchers speculated that this finding reflects the additional time provided and the benefits of participation in the debriefing session. The learners who played the game claimed it helped them learn new vocabulary and that the presentation of vocabulary contextualized within physical spaces in the game helped to facilitate understanding of the TL culture. As was the case in the first study, the control group expressed greater confidence in their form of instruction compared to the experimental group. However, the analysis revealed that in contrast to the control group, the experimental group invested more mental effort, found the assessment less challenging, and showed greater gains in vocabulary retention. The control group also found the homework to be more difficult than the experimental group. In a finding that suggests playing the game enhanced vocabulary transfer, data showed that this latter group produced longer and more lexical dense assessment essays than its peers. The researchers claimed that in order to maximize the potential of this type of game learner training should be provided, and that the game would be most effective when integrated with related classroom activities and homework assignments.

The researchers acknowledged that the duration of the project and small number of participants constituted limitations. Although these factors limit the generalizability of the findings, the design of this research also has a number of strengths. The researchers utilized a control group and, in addition, investigated the gameplay of beginner-level learners: As this discussion shows, research involving this type of learner is infrequent in the literature. Further beneficial features include use of a follow-up study and in-class debriefing. Furthermore, the contradictory nature of some of the learner feedback is important, as it draws attention to the limits on learner self-reporting.

Recent Research on the Use of Computer Games in CALL: Significant Findings

The analysis in this chapter highlights the fact that a major area of work on the use of computer games in CALL has focused on the use of simulation games. As table 6.1 shows, the discussion draws attention to a number of significant findings. Studies on the use of *The Sims* by Coleman (2002), Miller and Hegelheimer (2006), and Ranalli (2008), demonstrate the viability of using this type of commercial game in CALL involving intermediate-level EFL learners. Findings reported by the above researchers draw attention to the benefits of closely integrating game-based activities into a regular course. This body of work provides empirical evidence that significant gains in vocabulary can be achieved when simulation games are integrated in a pedagogically appropriate manner. Research suggests that this genre of

Table 6.1 Significant findings on the use of simulation games in CALL

Positive findings	*Negative findings*
Commercial simulation games are viable tools for use in CALL with intermediate-level EFL learners	Need for teacher assistance for lower level learners and inexperienced gamers
Significant gains in TL vocabulary	No gains in listening comprehension reported
Debriefing provides valuable insights in learner experiences and attitudes	Aspects of game play can be challenging for lower level learners
Use of supplementary materials and problem solving tasks supports collaboration and TL use	Participation frequently dependent on game subject matter being aligned with learner interests
Learner awareness of writing for an audience can be fostered	
Broadly positive learner attitudes	

game is more effective when combined with carefully designed supplementary materials and group work. The above studies further indicate that the use of authentic problem solving tasks that are based on game content facilitates collaboration, and the production of coherent TL output. Coleman's innovative research appears particularly noteworthy in this regard, as it emphasizes the benefits of this approach in raising beginner-level learner awareness of writing for an audience. The work of this researcher also highlights the insights into learner attitudes that can be obtained through participation in debriefing. Less encouraging findings are reported in terms of skills development. For example, the study conducted by Anderson et al. (2008) showed no significant gains in listening comprehension after play in *America's Army*. Moreover, the learner feedback reported in this study mirrors findings from other research (Ranalli 2008) indicating that although the majority of learners have positive attitudes toward simulation games, for lower level learners, and inexperienced gamers, play can be demanding. The above research suggests that in order to encourage active and meaningful participation a game's subject matter should appeal to learner interests. The research analyzed in this chapter further shows that the learning curve associated with this type of game frequently requires extensive teacher assistance (Ranalli 2008).

Another significant focus of research work on computer games in CALL has been the use of role-playing games. The discussion in this chapter has shown that the bulk of current studies have been conducted on network-based role-playing games such as MMORPGs. Researchers have investigated the use of commercial and modified MMORPGs along with purpose-built learning environments that incorporate this type of game. As table 6.2 shows, as is the case with research on simulation games, a range of positive findings are reported. Research shows that commercial MMORPGs such as *Ever Quest 2* and *World of Warcraft* are viable tools for CALL projects involving intermediate- and advanced-level learners, in both in-school and out-of-school settings. Studies confirm that participation in role-playing games elicits the production of TL output (Piirainen-Marsh and Tainio 2009; Rankin, Gold, and Gooch 2006; Reinders and Wattana 2011; Thorne 2008). Moreover, the work of Rankin, Gold, and Gooch (2006), and Reinders and Wattana (2011), demonstrates that for intermediate- and advanced-level EFL learners, TL output increases over time. This phenomenon may, in part, reflect the effectiveness of participation in training and debriefings. A further possible explanation may lie in the learners increasing familiarity. In less positive findings, Reinders and Wattana (2011) report that the learners in their study produced a simplified register that contained frequent errors that were not corrected. In addition, the quality of TL output in their research was variable. Moreover,

Table 6.2   Significant findings on the use of role-playing games in CALL

Positive findings	Negative findings
Both commercial and modified MMORPGs are viable tools for CALL projects involving intermediate- and advanced-level learners in both formal and informal settings	Beginner-level learners frequently find MMORPGs challenging
Participation in both commercial and purpose-built MMORPGs by intermediate- and advanced-level learners elicits the production of TL output and social interaction	Risk of cognitive overload
Training and debriefing supports learner participation	Production of a simplified register
Limited evidence for gains in vocabulary	Quality of TL output variable
Reading comprehension improved	Frequent absence of error correction
Learner motivation enhanced	
Presence of constructs identified in sociocultural SLA, including collaborative dialogue, zones of proximal development, and language socialization	
Variables such as prior knowledge, and network speeds influence learner behavior and attitudes	
Broadly positive learner attitudes	
Enjoyment	
Willingness to communicate enhanced	

accuracy and complexity did not improve over the three game sessions. However, this finding is unsurprising given the limited duration of the study. The findings reported by Rankin, Gold, and Gooch (2006), and Reinders and Wattana (2011), draw attention to the problems experienced by lower-level learners, and suggest that both commercial and modified MMORPGs present a challenging environment for learners of low proficiency and confidence levels. The positive results on vocabulary learning reported by Rankin, Gold, and Gooch (2006) are noteworthy and mirror findings from research on simulation games. However, as was noted previously, the limitations of this study make the findings challenging to generalize.

Studies reported by Thorne (2008) and Piirainen-Marsh and Tainio (2009) provide evidence to suggest that many constructs identified as beneficial in the sociocultural account of SLA such as collaborative dialogue involving assistance, language socialization, and interaction in zones of proximal development appear relevant to understanding language development in MMORPGs, and other types of role-playing games. However, as the analysis conducted in this chapter shows, both of these studies are subject to limitations. For example, Thorne's descriptive research involved only one learner, and the work conducted by Piirainen-Marsh and Tainio did not explore acquisition directly. Nonetheless, taken together, these studies suggest that this type of game may provide a context for purposeful and motivating social interaction in the TL that provides conditions conducive to SLA. The work reported by Suh, S. Kim, and N. Kim (2010) though not undertaken from any explicit theoretical perspective on SLA is nonetheless valuable, as it represents one of the largest studies undertaken to date on the use of a MMORPG designed specifically to facilitate language learning. As was noted previously, this research is significant for its longitudinal nature, use of a control group, range of data sources, and rigorous empirical approach to data analysis. Although it was found that there was no significant difference in learning achievement between the experimental and the control group, this study establishes that the learners who played the MMORPG achieved higher scores in reading, writing, and listening. Moreover, in contrast to the majority of studies this research presents valuable findings that identify a range of variables that may influence learning. The researchers identify prior knowledge, motivation, and network speed as the key variables that influence learning. A noteworthy feature of the research on MMORPGs is that learner feedback particularly from intermediate- and advanced-level learners is broadly positive in the majority of studies. Positive aspects of MMORPGs identified in this body of work include enjoyment, opportunities for fluency practice, improved vocabulary knowledge, reading comprehension, and enhanced willingness to communicate (Rankin, Gold, and Gooch 2006; Reinders and Wattana 2011; Thorne 2008).

This chapter shows that a further important area of research work has concentrated on the use of MUVE-based games. As table 6.3 shows, this research has yielded a number of insights. The analysis of findings has established the viability of this type of game as an arena for CALL projects involving intermediate-level learners. The negative learner feedback reported by Johnson (2007) suggests that in order to elicit positive learner attitudes, game content should reflect expectations. In this context, the findings of Johnson's research further demonstrate that when MUVE-based games are designed based on player feedback, and are integrated into a comprehensive

Table 6.3   Significant findings on the use of MUVE-based games in CALL

Positive findings	Negative findings
MUVE-based games viable tools for CALL projects involving intermediate-level learners	Negative attitudes if game content does not meet learner expectations
Active participation	Errors not always corrected
Discourse management practice	
Production of complex TL output during quests	
Social interaction	
Collaborative TL interaction involving negotiation of meaning and scaffolding	
Self and other-initiated correction	
Intercultural awareness facilitated	
Positive learner feedback	
Beneficial effects of learner training	

learning system, highly motivated learners view them as beneficial. The findings of the case study undertaken by Zheng et al. (2009), though based on a small number of learners, are nonetheless encouraging. The detailed analysis carried out in this study draws attention to the benefits of participation in MUVE-based games with young learners in informal out-of-school settings. Significant positive findings include evidence that collaborative TL interaction involving negotiation of meaning, reciprocal action during peer scaffolding, and correction occurred. Moreover, this research provides useful insights into how the communication environment elicited active participation and provided valuable opportunities for practice in managing TL discourse. *Quest Atlantis* enabled learners to express their identities in the TL and raised their intercultural awareness though repeated goal-based social interaction. The presence of self and other-initiated correction represents a positive finding. The largely positive learner feedback emphasizes the opportunities for TL use and development provided by this type of game. In findings that mirror the positive results reported by Zheng et al. (2009), Liang (2011) provides evidence that the upper intermediate-level learners in her experimental research assumed an active role in the management of their discourse during gameplay in *Erie Isle*. Moreover, they consistently engaged in the production of a wide range of complex TL output during quests. As was the case in the research reported by Zheng et al. (2009), the learners undertook dialogue involving the negotiation of meaning, and scaffolding. In a less positive finding, it was found that the learners did not always correct their errors. However, they produced complex TL output incorporating a wide range of discourse involving language play. The positive findings reported in Liang's research further reflect the benefits of providing training.

As may be observed in table 6.4, the studies analyzed in this chapter show mixed results regarding the use of a variety of other game types in learner-based projects. In the research conducted by Stubbs (2003), the participants reported that playing a typing-based shooter game was fun. The anecdotal nature of this study highlights the need for further research on this type of game. Learner interest and enjoyment were identified as beneficial aspects of gameplay in a 3D adventure game (Chen and Yang 2011), sports (deHaan 2005), and rhythm game (deHaan, Reed, and Kuwada 2010). Chen and Yang (2011) draw attention to the sense of achievement engendered by completing challenging game tasks and the exposure to colloquial usages that are frequently not found in many language classrooms. Their research also draws attention to positive feedback, with learners claiming improvements in listening, reading, and vocabulary skills after playing an adventure game. deHaan's (2005) research though subject to the limitations outlined previously, provides limited evidence suggesting that listening comprehension, vocabulary recall, and pronunciation may be improved by a sports game that provides extensive exposure to the TL in both written and aural forms. In terms of this later factor, the empirical results reported by deHaan, Reed,

Table 6.4 Significant findings on the use of shooter, rhythm, sports, 3D, and text-based adventure games

Positive findings	Negative findings
Learner feedback indicates interest and enjoyment	Risk of cognitive overload
Limited evidence for enhanced vocabulary recall, and improvements in listening, pronunciation, and reading	Necessity for learning scaffolds when using games designed for native speakers
Sense of achievement	Need for learner control of game elements
Exposure to colloquial usages	
Participation in orientation and debriefing are beneficial	
Awareness of the TL culture enhanced	

and Kuwada (2010) show that repeated playing of a rhythm game may, to a degree, support vocabulary recall. However, the above studies demonstrate the cognitively demanding nature of sports and rhythm games. deHaan (2005) emphasizes that learner ability to control aspects of a game such as the dialogue can significantly enhance learner performance. The findings reported by Chen and Yang (2011) appear to support this assertion, as the learners in this study identified a lack of learner control of over important elements of game content, such as, for example, character dialogues, as a problematic feature of the games' design. This finding mirrors results reported by deHaan, Reed, and Kuwada (2010). This large-scale study is significant in that its results indicate that, for many participants, playing a rhythm game induced cognitive overload. This result highlights the need for additional studies in order to clarify the suitability of this type of game for use in CALL. These researchers noted the necessity of providing scaffolds when using games such as rhythm games that are designed for use by native speakers. The study carried out by Neville, Shelton, and McInnis (2009) draws attention to potential benefits of using a text-based adventure game. Although these researchers note that the learners found this type of game challenging, they provided evidence that playing the game supported the production of TL output, vocabulary recall, and raised awareness of the TL culture. The findings of this research further suggest that learning outcomes may be maximized when learners participate in orientations and debriefing sessions.

This chapter draws attention to common themes that are reflected in both the early and current literature. A number of encouraging findings are reported across studies that echo in certain respects, claims made in early work that was examined in the previous chapter. The discussion shows that a majority of studies suggest that with the exception of rhythm games, many types of commercial, adapted, and purpose-built computer games are viable tools for CALL projects. The existing literature suggests that most of the games examined in this chapter are suitable for use with learners possessing intermediate and advances levels of proficiency. Results on the use of games with beginner-level learners are mixed. The majority of studies suggest that more complex games such as commercial MMORPGs and rhythm games, appear unsuitable for this learner group (deHaan, Reed, and Kuwada 2010; Rankin, Gold, and Gooch 2006). However, work reported by Coleman (2002) shows that good results can be obtained when beginner-level learners work in groups with active teacher support. Taken as a whole, the data analyzed in this discussion demonstrates that playing various types of computer games can facilitate the production of TL output. The majority of studies indicate that playing a variety of computer games elicits active learner participation and enhances motivation (Liang 2011; Piirainen-Marsh and Tainio 2009; Thorne 2008; Zheng et al. 2009). Furthermore, data from a number of studies suggests that a range of computer games can be used to enhance vocabulary learning (Miller and Hegelheimer 2006; Neville, Shelton, and McInnis 2009; Ranalli 2008; Rankin, Gold, and Gooch 2006). In regard to this aspect of language learning, simulation games and role-playing games appear particularly promising. The literature also contains evidence that these games offer valuable opportunities to engage in forms of collaborative interaction that are identified as beneficial in both cognitive and sociocultural accounts of SLA. The data indicates that the real-time problem-based nature of the interaction in these games over extended periods facilitates collaboration, socialization, negotiation of meaning, and the operation of zones of proximal development (Piirainen-Marsh and Tainio 2009; Thorne 2008; Zheng et al. 2009).

A further noteworthy trend across the majority of both early and more recent research is the prevalence of positive learner attitudes (Rankin, Gold, and Gooch 2003; Stubbs 2003; Thorne 2008; Zheng et al. 2009). Research is consistent in highlighting the enjoyment and sense of challenge engendered by many types of computer games used in CALL (Rankin, Gold, and Gooch 2006; Reinders and Wattana 2011). Learners consistently identify the active engagement and interest engendered by games and emphasize the fact that they consider the opportunities for TL use to be valuable in terms of developing aspects of fluency including reading, listening, and writing skills (Chen and Yang 2011; Rankin, Gold, and Gooch 2006; Reinders and Wattana 2011). The feedback examined in this discussion highlights the importance of game content meeting learner expectations, and the benefits of engaging learners with games that provide players with control over aspects of game features such as, for example, character dialogues (Chen and Yang 2011; Johnson 2007). Moreover, the findings of several studies suggest that when using commercial games learner performance can be significantly improved when game-based learning is integrated into the wider curriculum, and when teacher-produced scaffolds in the form of supplementary materials based on game content are available (Coleman 2002; Liang 2011; Miller and Hegelheimer 2006; Reinders and Wattana 2011). In this context, the literature further confirms the findings of early research, namely, the important influence of learning training on performance, and the potentially valuable opportunities for learning provided by participation in debriefing (Anderson et al. 2008; Coleman 2002; deHaan 2005; Miller and Hegelheimer 2006; Neville, Shelton, and McInnis 2009; Ranalli 2008).

Although the bulk of studies analyzed in this chapter report positive findings researchers also echo concerns raised in early work that were noted in the previous chapter. A consistent theme in recent research is the need for educators to acknowledge the learning curve faced by players of more complex games (Anderson et al. 2008; deHaan 2005). Research indicates that when using games in CALL, educators must carefully consider the risks of exposure to limited game-specific registers. The results reported by deHaan, Reed, and Kuwada (2010) are important, as although they are the product of only one study, they provide credible evidence to suggest that the cognitive demands placed on learners by a commercial rhythm game may make this game type unsuitable for use with many learner groups. Another concern noted in research is the variable quality of the TL produced by learners (Reinders and Wattana 2011). Furthermore, a number of studies reviewed in this chapter indicate no significant differences in learner performance between experimental and control groups (Anderson et al. 2008; Suh, S. Kim, and N. Kim 2010). Additional problematic findings include the prevalence of errors and limited evidence for correction (Liang 2011; Reinders and Wattana 2011). These later findings highlight the risk of the incorporation of incorrect forms. Research further suggests that in order to maximize learning outcomes educators would be well advised to closely align game selection to learner needs, expectations, and proficiency level (deHaan, Reed, and Kuwada 2010; Johnson 2007).

This discussion demonstrates that while research work has expanded significantly over the past ten years there are significant issues with the current research base. Unfortunately, large-scale studies remain infrequent in the literature. A noteworthy feature of the majority of studies analyzed here is their small-scale, exploratory nature (Anderson et al. 2008; deHaan 2005; Piirainen-Marsh and Tainio 2009; Rankin, Gold, and Gooch 2006; Stubbs 2003; Thorne 2008). The limited duration of the majority of recent projects draws attention to the urgent need for longitudinal studies. As the analysis conducted in this chapter shows, there is a need for research that employs mixed methods, control groups, draws on previous work, accounts for the possible influence of novelty, and that is firmly grounded in theories of SLA. Additional research that adopts both quantitative and qualitative approaches to data analysis is necessary, as this offers the prospect of shedding new light on the complex nature of learning with games and their potential in CALL. A further issue with current research work is that it has tended to investigate only certain areas. Moreover, most studies have only investigated a narrow range of variables. To date, research is heavily focused on vocabulary learning, and the investigation of learner attitudes. Although work in these areas is important and continues, at present, there remains a need for studies that explore other areas associated with language learning such as, for example, grammatical development. Furthermore, in common with early work, in many, though not all studies, there is a heavy and largely uncritical reliance on learner self-reporting. The contradictory nature of the learner feedback reported by Neville, Shelton, and McInnis (2009) emphasizes the need for researchers to be aware of the limitations on learner self-reporting. Another striking feature of current research is, with the exception of the study undertaken by Suh, S. Kim, and N. Kim (2010), there is a general absence of comparative work. A key area in future research on the use of games in CALL lies in comparing the effectiveness of this approach to other forms of delivery.

Although current research is subject to the above limitations, this chapter draws attention to a number of welcome developments. These include the emergence of well-designed studies on specific game genres that draw on previous relevant work, and that are firmly grounded in SLA research (Liang 2011; Miller and Hegelheimer 2006; Piirainen-Marsh and Tainio 2009; Ranalli 2008; Thorne 2008; Zheng et al. 2009). This phenomenon represents an important advance on early work. The broadly positive findings reported in these studies demonstrate the increasing influence of systematic and rigorous theory-led approaches to development work and research.

The critical examination of the recent literature on the use of computer games in language education conducted in this chapter draws attention to broadly encouraging findings. Analysis reveals that although research is subject to limitations, and is not yet conclusive, the majority of existing studies highlight the potential benefits of using computer games in CALL. Although research is expanding, researchers have consistently emphasized the urgent need for additional longitudinal studies (Reinders and Wattana 2011; Suh, S. Kim, and N. Kim 2010). Moreover, this chapter draws attention to the need for case studies that are conducted with reference to theories that stress the social nature of language acquisition. The analysis in this chapter demonstrates that of the games currently under investigation, research suggests that MMORPGs appear promising arenas for language learning. In order to contribute to the literature, the following chapter will report the findings of a longitudinal case study that investigates from the perspective of social SLA research, learner gameplay in a MMORPG.

CHAPTER 7

The Use of a MMORPG in CALL: A Case Study

MMORPGs and Language Learning

As noted in chapter 1, research on the use of technological innovations in CALL is subject to limitations. The need for additional theory-led studies that address the issues raised in prior work is a consistent theme in the literature (Chapelle 2009; Salaberry 2001). Researchers have argued for increased linkages between innovations in SLA theory and research work in CALL (Chapelle 2004, 2005; Gutierrez 2003; Salaberry 1999). In this context, developments in SLA theory that emphasize the benefits of engaging learners in TL interaction are becoming increasingly influential. However, as the discussion in chapter 1 demonstrates, the impact of these developments on the CALL literature is limited. As Salaberry observes when discussing potentially valuable areas for further research in CALL:

> I argue that one of the most understudied and perhaps underrated consequences of the use of new technologies has been the interaction among learners generated by activities based on the use of new technologies. This interaction is what I proposed (Salaberry, 1999) should be considered one of the central components of a research agenda for CALL in the years to come. (Salaberry 2001, 51–52)

Chapters 4 and 6 draw attention to the potential of MMORPGs as venues for CALL. Current work, though preliminary in nature, suggests that participation in MMORPGs can provide opportunities for learners to engage in forms of TL interaction that are hypothesized as beneficial in the social account of SLA. As the discussion in chapter 6 shows, positive findings identified in the literature include collaborative dialogue, zones of proximal development, and language socialization (Reinders and Wattana 2011; Thorne 2008). Although current research on MMORPGs has provided encouraging findings, it is limited in scope and shares many of the issues associated with other areas of CALL research. Researchers claim that while this type of game appears promising there are problems with current research as Suh, S. Kim, and N. Kim state:

> Research on MMORPG applications in education tend to be conceptual or anecdotal in nature. (Suh, S. Kim, and N. Kim 2010, 371)

Researchers emphasize that additional research is required in this area (Rankin, Gold, and Gooch 2006; Thorne 2008). Reinders and Wattana (2011, 24) point out the need for more studies and propose a wide-ranging approach. The necessity for additional research is a theme taken up by Reinhardt and Sykes, who identify the following areas of as being of particular interest:

> Research must continue to examine game design, in-game behaviors, and learning outcomes. As has been discussed in previous work...task design (quests), interaction (player-to-player and player-to-non-player character), and feedback type and presentation are especially noteworthy areas in which to begin. (Reinhardt and Sykes 2012, 45)

Thorne (2008) asserts that exploring learner-social interaction in MMORPGs from the perspective of sociocultural theory may provide valuable insights. As the literature indicates that more work is needed on learner interaction in MMORPGs this research investigates this factor. Moreover, as learner attitudes have not been subject to extensive analysis this study will also focus on this area.

Methodology

Research Questions

The literature on the use of MMORPGs in CALL reports encouraging preliminary findings, and draws attention to the need for additional longitudinal studies that explore learner in-game behavior from the perspective of interactionist SLA research. This study adds to the literature on the under-researched areas of learner-player interaction and attitudes. In line with the necessity for theory-led work expressed in the literature, social interactionist SLA research informs the data analysis. This qualitative study will aim to answer the following research questions:

1. During game play in a commercial MMORPG do learners engage in forms of TL interaction that are identified as beneficial in social accounts of SLA? If so, what types of interaction do they undertake?
2. What are learner attitudes toward gameplay in a commercial MMORPG?

Research Design

In order to answer the above questions, this longitudinal qualitative research draws on a case study that incorporates discourse analysis of learner in-game interaction as the primary research tool. Discourse analysis was selected as previous research on the use of MMORPGs in CALL demonstrates that this tool provides valuable insights into learner behavior (Reinders and Wattana 2011; Thorne 2008). A case study was adopted for a number of reasons. The use of a case study enabled the incorporation of a variety of data sources into the research design including chat transcripts, observation, questionnaires, interviews, and field notes. This facilitated triangulation and the collection of a richer set of data sources than could be provided by other means (Merriam 1998). The use of a case study design further enabled the interaction of individual learners and small groups to be studied in-depth over a sustained period. The literature indicates that this aspect of case studies (Chapelle and Duff 2003) supports the identification of significant themes and patterns across the data and facilitates both micro and macro level perspectives on learner behavior.

Participants

The volunteer participants in this research were ten undergraduate EFL students based at a university in western Japan. As table 7.1 shows, responses to a pre-study questionnaire indicated that seven were female and that all of the participants were native speakers of Japanese. The learners ranged in age from 20 to 23 years old. The participants claimed intermediate levels of English proficiency. Recent test scores provided by nine of the participants indicated proficiency levels ranged from lower to advanced intermediate. Of the advanced-level learners, two stated that they had lived in both the United States and United Kingdom for one year. Another learner studied in the United Kingdom for nine months. The remaining learners indicated

Table 7.1 Learner responses to the pre-study questionnaire

Learner	Gender	Age	English proficiency level	Experience of playing Wonderland
Learner 1	Female	20	Intermediate	None
Learner 2	Female	20	Intermediate	None
Learner 3	Female	20	Intermediate	None
Learner 4	Female	20	Intermediate	None
Learner 5	Female	20	Intermediate	None
Learner 6	Female	20	Intermediate	None
Learner 7	Female	20	Intermediate	None
Learner 8	Male	23	Intermediate	None
Learner 9	Male	20	Intermediate	None
Learner 10	Male	20	Intermediate	None

that they had never been overseas. Seven learners claimed they seldom played computer games. One learner stated that they played computer games regularly while another two learners claimed that they never played computer games. None of the participants claimed any prior experience of playing the MMORPG utilized in this research.

MMORPG Investigated in This Research

The MMORPG used in this research *Wonderland* (http://wl.igg.com/) is character-based and draws on Japanese animation themes. In common with other MMORPGs, the above game presents players with access to a high quality virtual world that is populated by player avatars and game generated non-player characters. In this 2D game players can communicate in real time by means of an online chat tool. The chat system provides both public and private chat channels. Players can select from a number of predesigned emoticons on an on-screen toolbar that enable their avatars to display a range of emotional states such as happiness, surprise, and sadness. In addition, player avatars are customizable and can perform physical actions, traverse virtual space, and gather objects that can be added to personal inventories. The interface provides access to a hypertext link that when selected enables a player to offer friendship to others. When an offer of friendship is accepted players can form teams to undertake quests. The game also provides email and emote systems. The game adopts a novel story line whereby new players are shipwrecked on a desert island. The primary goal of players is to progress to higher levels in the hierarchy, an activity known as *leveling up*. To achieve this objective, players are required to undertake a variety of quests. Quests can be undertaken individually or in teams and frequently involve following instructions from non-player characters. Typical quests encountered by players include engaging in combat with monsters, trading virtual commodities, retrieving specific items, and developing special skills. On reaching higher status levels, players have the opportunity to join guilds that enable individuals to cooperate with peers in the development of game-specific skills and abilities. This game was selected as it provides an open-access communication environment. Moreover, it is designed to facilitate social interaction. Extensive online player support is provided in a web site that incorporates help and FAQ pages. A further valuable feature of the web site is access to extensive player forums.

Orientation and Debrief

This research was undertaken in two stages during the fall semester of 2011. As research studies emphasize the need to provide training in the use of advanced games (Coleman 2002; Reinders and Wattana 2011), prior to the main phase an orientation was initiated. This was initially planned for two one-and-a-half-hour sessions held one week apart. The first orientation was designed to provide a thorough overview of the game story line, provide training, test the practicalities of using the MMORPG in an institutional environment, and obtain learner feedback. During this session the learners were introduced to the game FAQ pages and player forums. At this stage, a number of issues arose. In the first session, it became apparent that the original venue chosen for this research, a computer classroom located at the student's university was unsuitable, due to the presence of network firewalls. For the second session, the venue was changed to a computer lab with open access to the Internet. The researcher observed that in this session the two lower-level learners who were novice gamers, experienced persistent difficulties. In informal discussions held during the debriefing these learners expressed the desire for more training. In response to this request, a further training session was held for all participants.

Data Sources and Procedures

In order to support triangulation, multiple sources of data were collected and analyzed. The researcher used screen-capture software to record the real time in-game interaction of the participants. Text chat data was collected from six weekly sessions that constitute the main phase of this research. During each of the sessions the learners were requested to play the game for approximately 70 minutes. An additional source of data was obtained through researcher observation. During the sessions, the researcher observed the gameplay and significant instances of learner behavior were recorded in field notes. Participant attitudes were investigated by means of a post-study questionnaire administered by the researcher after the final session. The above sources of data was supplemented by learner reports submitted after the final session and informal semi-structured interviews conducted by the researcher after the final game session. The learners provided written consent for the collection, reproduction, and analysis of the data.

Findings

Analysis of the data reveals findings that relate to the research questions. The discussion will first provide an overview of the communication context. This will be followed by an analysis of learner-player interaction and an examination of learner attitudes. The discussion focuses on analyzing illustrative excerpts of significant chat and email interaction recorded during gameplay in *Wonderland*. In order to provide for anonymity, each learner will be identified through use of a unique pseudonym, for example, *learner 1*. Other players are identified by use of pseudonyms, such as *player 1*. The target language output produced by the learners is presented unedited. However, in order to highlight significant interaction, system messages and turns not related to the interaction at hand are not provided.

Learner In-Game Interaction:
Communication Context

The interactional context provided by *Wonderland* presented the participants, who were novice players of this particular game, with a number of challenges. In order to progress and communicate effectively, players must control their personal avatars and follow text messages that can scroll rapidly in the on-screen textbox. At the same time they are required to interact with other players and game-generated non-player characters. Moreover, in common with most other MMORPGs, players must make sense of messages in a communication context where many of the cues that influence communication in face-to-face contexts such as age and gender are either absent or greatly reduced. In order to progress in the game, players must also come to understand this particular discourse community, including its specific communication norms. In this context, the learners had to familiarize themselves with a unique game-specific register that is frequently utilized by experienced high-level players. An example of interaction displaying this register relating to the sale and purchase of game items necessary for a specific quest drawn from the chat data collected in session six is reproduced in excerpt 1:

1. 1 Learner 1: hi
   2 Press Alt+1 to recover HP and Sp gradually
   3 Player 1: cuss burst im fire pm me
   4 Player 1: cuss burst im fire pm me
   5 Player 2: Gold Eagle Totem, Blue monster clothes
   6 Learner 2: please let me join ur team
   7 Player 2: Escape Button pm me for offer
   8 Player 3: Buying 4 bombs pm me
   9 Player 4: tar ☺ pls pm me ty-

As the above interaction shows, the register that frequently operates in *Wonderland* is somewhat complex and contains a number of distinct features. These include player (lines 1, 3, 4, 5, 6, 7, 8, and 9) and system generated messages (line 2), the extensive use of abbreviations (lines 3, 4, 6, 7, 8, and 9) that often contain game-specific meanings such as the ubiquitous "pm me" meaning contact me using the in-game mailing system (lines 3, 4, 7, 8 and 9), and the use of emoticons designed to display emotional states (line 9). A significant feature of the data was that with two exceptions, the learners were able for the most part, to deal with the potentially challenging communication environment. Observation revealed that as this research progressed the participants came to display a degree of competency in using the communication systems provided including text chat, email, and emotes. They were also able to follow instructions provided by non-player characters. As the following discussion shows, although the participants encountered problems, they were able to play the game and collaborate, while also engaging in social interaction in the TL with other players.

Making Friends and Forming Teams

The review of the literature conducted in chapter 6 indicates that participation in MMORPGs promotes social interaction (Thorne 2008). A noteworthy feature of the chat data was extensive evidence of social interaction. The data shows that the learners engaged in TL interaction involving forms of collaboration. Analysis reveals that from the fourth session onward the learners took an active role in initiating and managing their interaction. One form of collaborative TL interaction elicited by participation in the gameplay was the process of making friends. As stated at an earlier stage of this discussion, *Wonderland* is designed to facilitate teamwork and one means to support team formation is for players to offer each other friendship. If an offer of friendship is accepted then players can then form teams in order to collaborate on future activities such as quests. The data showed that in each of the sessions learners initiated offers of friendship to other players. A typical instance of a learner offering friendship occurred in session five:

> 2. 1 Learner 6: hey
>   2 Player 1: yes?
>   3 Learner 6: can i be your friend?
>   4 Player 1: sure ☺
>   5 Learner 6: thank you

In excerpt 2, learner 6 attempts to attract the attention of another player through use of an interjection. In the next turn, the intended recipient responds with a question. This prompt response elicits a friendship request that incorporates politeness. The other player responds positively in an informal utterance containing an emoticon designed to display happiness. In the next turn, learner 6 again utilizes politeness to express gratitude and signal that the offer has been accepted. In following turns, learner 6 accepted an offer to be a team leader and was observed undertaking a quest in collaboration with player 1.

Off-Quest Discussion

The literature on learner interaction in chat rooms indicates that off-task discussion plays an important role in facilitating the operation of communities of practice (Darhower 2002). Research on the use of text chat in CALL projects has further confirmed that learners use a range of utterances designed to signal attention, interest, surprise, and encouragement (Zheng et al. 2009). These utterances, known as continuers, are an important means to establish and maintain the social cohesion necessary for collaborative interaction in the absence of social context cues (Foster and Ohta 2005). Observation indicated that throughout the sessions the learners were highly focused on completing the quests. However, it was found that the participants engaged in social interaction involving use of continuers that was not directly related to the conduct of the quests.

Analysis revealed that off-quest interaction involving use of continuers occurred in all of the sessions. An instance of this type of interaction on the local chat channel involving three participants and a player from China was observed in session seven:

3. 1 Learner 8: i found your dog.
   2 Player 2: ☺☺
   (two lines of text)
   3 Player 2: my deskmate want to live in Japan
   (five lines of text)
   4 Learner 3: really? i'm grad to hear that
   5 Player 2: which city do you want to live in?
   6 Learner 9: i live in osaka japan
   7 Learner 9: osaka is very good place
   8 Learner 9: Come to japan!
   9 Learner 8: I live in Kyoto, do u know?
   10 Learner 9: Come to osaka!
   11 Player 2: yeah
   12 Player 2: but i don't know your language
   13 Learner 9: in osaka you should eat Takoyaki
   14 Player 2: what's that?
   15 Learner 9: Don't worry. you can use Chinese in japan

In the opening turn of the above interaction, learner 8 signals that player 2's pet dog has been found. In a prompt response, player two uses two emoticons designed to display happiness. After a brief delay, player 2 makes a statement directed to other players in the immediate vicinity. After five turns scroll, learner 3 responds with a continuer designed to display surprise and interest. Player 2 then attempts to elicit feedback from another player through the use of a question. Although this utterance appears directed at learner 3, this effort meets with a prompt response from two other learners. In line 6, learner 9 responds, and in the following turn provides additional information. In the next turn, this learner attempts to move the interaction forward by the use of a continuer that incorporates an invitation. Learner 8 then rejoins the discussion with a statement that confirms their location. This utterance is followed by use of a continuer in the form of a comprehension check. In the next turn, player 9 utilizes another continuer to extend a further invitation to player 2. In the following turns, player 2 uses an informal exclamation to signal agreement and then expresses concern that they have no knowledge of Japanese. In response, learner 9 recommends a popular local food (*takoyaki*). Player 2 responds by signaling nonunderstanding. However, in the final turn of the above interaction learner 9 does not resolve this issue, instead they attempt to maintain the friendly atmosphere by expressing reassurance.

Interaction involving use of continuers that was not directly related to the conduct of the quests was identified across the sessions and played an important role in the management of the discourse. As the above excerpt shows, the use of continuers provided a means to signal interest and convey a positive cooperative attitude. Moreover, the frequent use of continuers contributed to the informal nature of much of the interaction, and enabled the participants to establish and maintain rapport. This type of social interaction created a context for continuation of the discourse, fostered social cohesion, and facilitated the maintenance of collaborative interpersonal relationships.

Collaboration Involving Assistance

In accounts of SLA informed by sociocultural theory, the assistance provided by more capable peers during interaction is perceived as playing a central role in learning (Lantolf 2000). As the discussion in chapter 6 shows there is evidence in the CALL literature suggesting that MMORPGs may provide a context conducive to the operation of collaborative dialogue (Thorne 2008). In this regard, a significant feature of the data was the presence of collaborative TL dialogue where the learners utilized requests. The data shows that learners took the initiative in making requests for assistance directed at other players. A frequent use related to specific locations required by quests and involved relatively brief interactions. An example of this phenomenon may be observed in excerpt 4 which occurred in session seven:

> 4. 1 Learner 5: Hi. Do you know where the cave is?
> 2 Player 3: cave is north of the village
> 3 Learner 5: thanks

In the above interaction, learner 5 first greets players in the immediate vicinity and then makes a request in the form of a question. This is met with a prompt response from player 3 who, in the next turn, provides appropriate assistance. In the following turn, learner 5 utilizes politeness in order to express gratitude.

On other occasions during quests, more lengthy interaction involving requests for assistance occurred over a sustained period. A typical instance of this phenomenon occurred in session nine during an interaction that took place on a private chat channel:

> 5. 1 Learner 3: Hi tat4
> 2 Player 4: hi
> (one line of text)

3 Learner 3: hows this game?
(three lines of text)
4 Player 4: good, u enjoying it?
5 Learner 3: yeah but i don't understand this game so well
(one line of text)
6 Learner 3: how do u become better i this game?
7 Player 4: what do u not understand?
8 Player 4: what is ur lvl?
9 Learner 3: lv4
10 Player 4: oh teehe
11 Player 4: well u gotta lvl up first
12 Player 4: go to that cave here
13 Player 4: and autowalk
14 Learner 3: which cave?
(two lines of text)
15 Player 4: hmm i show u
(two lines of text)
16 Learner 3: thank you
(one line of text)
17 Player 4: follow
(two lines of text)
18 Player 4: follow me
(one line of text)
19 Learner 3: ok where ar u?
20 Player 4: near u
21 Learner 3: oh you are here
(two lines of text)
22 Player 4: follow me
23 Learner 3: ok
(two lines of text)
24 Player 4: here
(one line of text)
25 Player 4: u kill those mobs
(one line of text)
26 Player 4: here
27 Learner 3: thank u !

In the opening turns of the above excerpt, learner 3 initiates the interaction with an exchange of greetings with player 4, and then engages in small talk concerning the game. This later interchange provides a context for the following interaction. In turn 5, learner 3 in an utterance that incorporates informal language and an abbreviation, signals limited understanding of the game. In the next turn, this learner makes a direct request for assistance in the form of a continuer that incorporates a confirmation check. In the next two turns, player 4 first elicits feedback on the nature of the problem, and then confirms their interlocutors' level in the game. In turn 11, this player offers appropriate advice on the necessity of leveling up and then after a display of humor designed to maintain the relaxed atmosphere suggests a move to a cave on the island. In turn 14, after a short delay learner 3 uses a continuer to request confirmation of the next location. After initial confusion this learner then expresses gratitude in an utterance incorporating politeness. At this stage of the interaction learner 3's avatar is observed following player 4 to the cave. In turn 19, learner 3 appears to lose sight of player 4's avatar and utilizes an informal utterance that contains an abbreviation in order to confirm the location of their interlocutor. In the following turns this issue is resolved. In turn 24, player 4 reveals their location, and in the next turn, provides assistance relating to the specific task required to level up, in this case, fighting monsters. In response, learner 3 expresses gratitude for the assistance through the use of an informal utterance containing politeness.

A further noteworthy instance of a learner requesting assistance occurred in session eight. This collaboration involved a learner requesting assistance from a more experienced player on ways to utilize a specific feature of the game, in this case, the variety of emoticons and emotes that are frequently used in *Wonderland* to display feedback regarding emotional states. Prior to this interaction, the avatar of learner 6 was observed approaching another player:

6. 1 Learner 6: hi dany26
   2 Player 5: its 96
   (four lines of text)
   3 Learner 6: oh sorry
   4 Player 5: hi ☺
   (one line of text)
   5 Learner 6: How are you dany96
   6 Player 5: fine
   (three lines of text)
   7 Learner 6: Where are you from?
   (one line of text)
   8 Learner 6: Im from japan
   (two lines of text)
   9 Player 5: oh really?
   (one line of text)
   10 Player 5: im from Malaysia

(three lines of text)
11 Learner 6: Oh, malasia?
(four lines of text)
12 Player 5: yea ☺
(one line of text)

The above excerpt begins with an exchange of informal greetings followed by off-quest interaction designed to establish and maintain a good atmosphere. In turn 7, learner 6 uses a continuer in the form of question designed to show interest and confirm the location of their interlocutor. In the following turn, this learner confirms their nationality. In turn 9, player 5 signals interest and in the next turn provides an appropriate response to the prior question. In the next turn, learner 6 uses a continuer in the form of a confirmation request in order to move the interaction forward. In response, player 5 confirms their location through the use of an informal utterance. This is followed by an emoticon designed to display a friendly positive attitude.

After a further ten lines of interaction involving small talk designed to build rapport, the following interaction unfolds:

23 Learner 6: do you play this game often>
24 Learner 6: ?
(twelve lines of text)
25 Player 5: i think its almost 4 year
(two lines of text)
26 Player 5: ☺
(two lines of text)
27 Player 5: ☺
(one line of text)
28 Learner 6: Wow!
(two lines of text)
29 Learner 6: i play this only 4 or 5 times
(three lines of text)
30 Learner 6: i don't know well what to do lol
31 Player 5: lol ☺

In turn 23, learner 6 attempts to move the interaction forward through use of a continuer designed to confirm the player status of their interlocutor. In the next turn, learner 6 promptly self-corrects. In turns 25 through 27, player 5 responds appropriately. In turn 28, learner 6 uses a continuer in the form of an interjection to express surprise at their interlocutor's considerable experience of the game. In the following turn, learner 6 makes a statement emphasizing their limited experience. This is accompanied in the next turn by humorous aside that incorporates use of the well know Internet acronym lol. This attempt to express humor is reciprocated in turn 31. In this turn, player 5 first repeats the same acronym and then uses an emoticon that is designed to display happiness and continue the humorous tone.

After five lines of text scroll, learner 6 in turn 37, utilizes a continuer in the form of a direct request for assistance regarding a significant feature of the prior interaction namely, player 5's frequent use of emoticons:

> 37 Learner 6: how do you type the smile mark?
> 38 Player 5: X
> 39 Player 5: and
> 40 Player 5: D
> 41 Learner 6: ☺
> 42 Player 5: look at the chat bar
> 43 Player 5: the right
> 44 Learner 6: wow thanks!
> (two lines of text)
> 45 Player 5: press it
> (two lines of text)
> 46 Player 5: do you see channel emotes
> (three lines of text)
> 47 Player 5: all the emotes you can do is there
> (three lines of text)
> 48 Learner 6: ☺ i got it!
> 49 Learner 6: thank you ☺
> 50 Player 5: cool
> 51 Player 5: have fun
> 52 Player 5: ☺
> 53 Player 5: ☺
> (three lines of text)
> 54 Learner 6: yeah you too

In turns 38 through 40, player 5 responds promptly to the request in feedback that contains helpful and accurate assistance regarding the commands required to display an emoticon. In turn 41, the use of an emoticon designed to display happiness signals that the advice has been followed. Researcher observation confirmed this conclusion as during this stage of the interaction the learner was observed utilizing these keyboard commands. In the following turns, player 5 supplies further advice on use of the prein-stalled emotes that are accessible on the game toolbar. In turn 48, learner 6 uses an emoticon followed by statement expressing understanding to demonstrate that the prior assistance has been successful. In the following turn, this learner utilizes politeness and an emoticon to express gratitude. In turn 51, player 5 signals that the interaction is coming to an end through use of an informal utterance. In the next 2 turns, this learner employs emoticons to facilitate a harmonious parting. After a brief delay, in turn 54 the interaction concludes with learner 6 expressing appreciation in an utterance incorporating informal language.

Nonresponse and Failed Communication

Analysis further reveals that although requests usually met with a helpful response there were instances when learner attempts to initiate interaction and obtain assistance were ignored or rebuffed. The following learner output from data collected from the early stages of session eight shows a learner making repeated and unsuccessful attempts on both private and public chat channels to elicit a response from other players:

7. 1 Player 6: Hey
   (four lines of text)
   2 Learner 8: How are you?
   3 Learner 8: My name is kogumanushi
   (one line of text)
   4 Learner 8: Please answer me!
   (three lines of text)
   5 Learner 8: hello>
   (two lines of text)
   6 Learner 8: hello
   (one line of text)
   7 Learner 8: How are you?

The data contained instances of appeals for assistance being ignored by other players as in the following excerpt from session four:

8. 1 Learner 10: help me
   (two lines of text)
   2 Learner 10: i don't know what to do

The data further shows that learner requests for assistance were, on occasion, rebuffed by high-level players as in the following example from session nine:

> 9. 1 Learner 4: hey could you help me
> 2 Player 7: im not in the mood to help ☺

The above phenomena occurred across the sessions and the reasons for this behavior are difficult to establish with certainty from the transcripts. One possible explanation for this finding may be the fact that certain areas in the game such as the village on the island were observed to be crowded with players. The presence of large numbers of players in specific locations raises the possibility that messages were missed as they scrolled rapidly. Another partial explanation may lie in the fact that the novice status of the learners was signaled by their TL use. During observation of the interaction the researcher noted that there was a distinct tendency for some high-level players to ignore those who did not make use of the particular game-specific register found in *Wonderland*. In this context, the extensive use of politeness by the participants may have led to avoidance. Moreover, it was observed that the participants, unlike higher status players, did not customize their avatars thus signaling their newbie status. In their feedback, the participants noted that they were sometimes ignored and learner claims regarding this issue will be examined at a later stage of this discussion.

Reciprocity

The data indicated that the learners not only received assistance, they also displayed reciprocity by providing assistance and advice to other players. An instance of this phenomenon occurred in session eight when during a quest learner 7 engaged in interaction with another player. Before the interaction, learner 7 was observed entering a shop and selling some game props. During this activity, this learner was observed accepting an offer of friendship from another player and the following interaction ensued on the in-game mailing system:

> 10. 1 Player 8: hi,, do you have other accounts?
> 2 Learner 7: no, i'm afraid not. why?
> 3 Player 8: i want to borrow
> 4 Learner 7: i am sorry i don't have one, why don't you make it for yourself?;)
> 5 Player 8: heeheheeh

6 Learner 7: i think my friend have two, so i'll ask her if she can lend you and let you know if she says its ok.
7 Player 8: tnxxx
8 Learner 7: your welcome;)
9 Player 8: i hope she can lend me one
10 Learner 7: is it ok if it may takoe
11 Learner 7: is it ok if it take some time to get her response?;)
12 Player 8: huh?do you a level 28 accountt,, buy it
13 Player 8: its ok,,,

In turn 1, player 8 opens the interaction with an informal greeting designed to display a friendly attitude. This is followed by a question concerning player accounts. Learner 7 utilizes politeness in a negative response and uses a continuer designed to establish the reason for the request. When this is provided in the next turn learner 7 apologizes and uses a continuer in the form of a suggestion. This utterance incorporates an emoticon to display humor and a cooperative attitude. When player 8 responds in a similar manner, learner 7 makes a helpful and appropriate suggestion on how to resolve the issue. In the next turn, player 8 expresses appreciation. This is reciprocated in the next turn where learner 7 uses politeness and an emoticon to maintain the friendly atmosphere and display rapport. In the following turn player 8 expresses hope that assistance will be forthcoming. In response, learner 7 first produces an erroneous utterance and then quickly self-corrects in a continuer incorporating a confirmation request that is also accompanied by use of an emoticon designed to display interest and signal that the interaction is ongoing. In the next turn, player 8 expresses surprise followed by a proposal. However, in the following turn this is promptly withdrawn. This move draws attention to the supportive nature of much of the interaction as player 8 appears eager to avoid the possibility of a misunderstanding.

The above interaction draws attention to a number of learner behaviors that were observed across the sessions. The learner adopts an active role during the interaction and produces accurate and coherent TL output that incorporates a range of discourse functions. Moreover, this participant, in common with the majority of the other learners, responds promptly and appropriately during the unfolding interaction displaying considerable discourse management skills. The above interaction though relatively brief, illustrates how the participants showed sensitivity toward their partners and made efforts to reduce the risks of misunderstanding occurring in a communication context where the cues that regulate face-to-face interaction are either absent or reduced. In an example of this phenomenon, during the potentially face threatening act of refusing a request the above learner makes appropriate use of politeness and humor in order to reduce the possibility of a negative response. Moreover, the consistent use continuers and emoticons demonstrate how the learners maintained social cohesion which in turn facilitated the operation of purposeful collaborative relationships.

Communication Problems

The transcript data contained evidence that the participants encountered communication problems involving the unique register used in the game. As was noted at an early stage of this discussion, game-specific vocabulary and abbreviations frequently occur during interaction between high-level players. Analysis indicates that the learners encountered communication problems relating to this aspect of the game particularly when communicating with more experienced higher status players. This aspect of the interaction appeared most prevalent in the early sessions as the learners came to terms with the communication environment. A typical instance occurred in session five during an interaction focusing on a quest between learner 2 and another player:

11. 1 Learner 2: I have 12 common glass, are u uk?
    2 Player 9: um... I will Take it with stack (1 stack=50pcs)
    (two lines of text)
    3 Learner 2: I don't know what is stack, ,
    4 Player 9: stack means....stack...
    5 Player 9: 1 stack means 50 pcs
    6 Learner 2: and..pcs?
    7 Player 9: pieces...
    8 Learner 2: ah, I see

In the above interaction, learner 2 and player 9 are involved in the trading of game items. In the opening turn, learner 2 makes an offer and uses a continuer in the form of a confirmation check. In the next turn, player 9 accepts the offer. After a brief delay, in turn 3, learner 2 signals that a communication problem has arisen over the meaning of the game term *stack*. In the following turns, player 9 provides an appropriate explanation. However, in turn 6 learner 2 signals through a repetition nonunderstanding of the game abbreviation *pcs* used in the previous turn. In turn 7, player 9 provides further relevant information. In the following turn, learner 2 in a continuer signals that the problem has been resolved successfully.

Although communication problems relating to the game's register were usually resolved quickly, the data also shows that, on occasion, technical issues prevented the resolution of such problems. An instance of this phenomenon occurred in session six:

12. 1 Learner 4: hey
     2 Learner 4: Fyn?
     3 Learner 4: do you know how to level up my character easiry?
     4 Player 10: burst it ☺
     5 Learner 4: what do you mean by burst?
     6 Learner 4: sorry i speak a little English.

Prior to the above excerpt, learner 4's avatar is observed approaching another player. In the first turn, this learner uses an informal greeting designed to display a friendly attitude. This is followed by use of the player's character name and a question mark designed to elicit a response. In turn 3, learner 4 uses a continuer in the form of a question. This utterance meets with a prompt response in the next turn, when player 10 in their feedback uses a game term in this case, the ubiquitous *burst*. In response, learner 4 signals through the use of a clarification request that a communication problem has arisen regarding the meaning of this term. In the next turn, this learner utilizes politeness to mitigate the effects of the intrusion. However, before player 10 can respond, the researcher observed that the above learner experienced a sudden systems failure and was unable to continue the interaction.

Learner Attitudes

In order to obtain feedback on learner attitudes, a post-study questionnaire was administered immediately after the final game session. The questionnaire consisted of 15 Likert items. In answering the participants were requested to select one response for each statement from the following options: one "strongly disagree," two "disagree," three "no opinion," four "agree," and five "strongly agree." Table 7.2 provides average responses for the eight participants who completed the questionnaire.

As can be observed in table 7.2, responses to the post-study questionnaire reveal a number of significant findings. The first five items were designed to elicit learner feedback on usability and technical issues encountered during this research. In response to statement 1, learner responses averaged 2.4, a finding indicating disagreement. Researcher observation confirmed that in the early sessions the participants encountered difficulties during gameplay. This finding is unsurprising as the learners were novice players. The general agreement reflected in responses to statements 2 and 3 draws attention to the specific nature of these difficulties. The response to statement 2 where

Table 7.2 Mean scores of participant responses to the post-study questionnaire

Statement	Mean
1. The game was easy to play	2.4
2. Sometimes I got lost	3.8
3. Sometimes I had computer problems	4.0
4. I could follow the conversation easily	2.3
5. Having an avatar made me feel more involved in the game	3.1
6. I found the quests interesting	3.6
7. I could learn new words and expressions	2.8
8. The English in the game was sometimes difficult to understand	2.5
9. I sometimes had trouble communicating	3.8
10. I could relax and did not worry about making mistakes	3.6
11. I could make friends in the game	2.9
12. Other players helped me when I had a problem	3.5
13. Other players sometimes ignored me	3.8
14. The game was fun	3.8
15. Playing the game was more interesting than a regular language class	4.0

the learners averaged 3.8 confirms that the majority experienced getting lost in the game. In the case of statement 3 responses averaged 4, indicating that the learners agreed with the assertion that they experienced computer problems during their gameplay. A partial source of these problems appeared linked to the technical requirements of the game. A feature of *Wonderland* that may have contributed to this finding was the requirement for periodic system upgrades. In the early stages of session four, it was observed that learner game time was reduced by the necessity to install automatic system upgrades. This phenomenon also occurred in session nine. As the previous discussion shows, a further technical issue that influenced learner participation involved system failures. The researcher noted that although not a frequent problem, on several occasions the interaction was interrupted for a period by a sudden systems failure. Responses to statement 4 averaged 2.3, this indicates disagreement with the assertion that the conversation was easy to follow. Researcher observation confirmed this phenomenon. The researcher noted that the lower-level learners in particular experienced difficulties in controlling their avatars while at the same following messages as they scrolled in real time. However, as this research progressed it became apparent that the majority of participants showed an increasing degree of comfort with the game. In response to statement 5 the learners averaged 3.1; this suggests that as a group, they had no opinion on whether the use of individual avatars enhanced the sense of involvement. However, an examination of individual responses reveals diversity in learner attitudes. The data shows that two learners disagreed, while a further three had no opinion. In contrast, three participants expressed agreement with this statement.

Statements 6 through 13 were designed to elicit learner views on specific aspects of participation in the gameplay. The learner responses to statement 6 averaged 3.6 indicating that most learners found the quests interesting. In the case of statement 7 learner responses averaged 2.8, this finding suggests that most learners did not acquire any new vocabulary. However, as the later discussion will show, other data appears to contradict this finding. Learner responses to statement 8 averaged 2.5, indicating general agreement that the language used in the game was, on occasion, difficult to understand. This confirms a finding first identified in the transcript analysis. Average responses to statements 9 and 10 were 3.8 and 3.6 respectively. These findings provide limited evidence suggesting that the learners encountered communication problems and that the communication environment may have, to a degree, reduced anxiety. Responses to statement 11 averaged 2.9 indicating that the learners had no strong opinions. However, this finding is contradicted by the transcript and observation data. This confirmed that across the sessions the learners were able to make friends and collaborate during quests. The contradictory nature of the learner feedback on social interaction is emphasized in the feedback to statements 12 and 13 where responses averaged 3.5. and 3.8 respectively. These findings mirror evidence identified in the transcript data showing that although there were occasions when the learners were ignored, they also received considerable assistance from other players. Statements 14 and 15 were designed to establish the level of enjoyment engendered and to compare participation in the sessions with a regular class. The learner feedback to these statements was positive. Responses to statement 14 averaged 3.8 highlighting general agreement that playing the game was fun. Moreover, the responses to statement 15 averaged 4.0. This finding confirms that the majority of the participants considered that playing the game was more interesting than participating in a regular language class.

In order to obtain additional data on attitudes the learners who completed the post-study questionnaire participated in informal interviews and submitted written reports. This learner feedback draws attention to a number of issues raised by the questionnaire. A number of the learners claimed that they encountered technical problems. These learners noted that occasional sudden systems failures and slow connection speeds hindered participation at times. This feedback mirrors findings reported in the literature (Suh, S. Kim, and N. Kim 2010). Several learners observed that the game could be very challenging and that they could have benefited from additional training. Researcher observation confirms the necessity for training particularly in the case of the lower-level learners. Although the majority of participants appeared comfortable with the game after the orientation and handled most aspects of the gameplay, the above learners continued to experience problems. In comments to the researcher these learners claimed that the game was difficult to play and that the interface was confusing leading to uncertainty regarding game objectives:

> It was very hard for me to play the game.
> There was too much information on the screen and that prevented me from knowing the situation well.

Additional problematic areas identified by these participants included keeping up with rapidly scrolling messages and difficulties in understanding the particular register used by experienced players. These themes were echoed in the feedback of other learners. In a report, a learner observed that the game register was on occasion problematic stating that:

> Sometimes incomprehensible sentences appeared one by one, and I had to scroll several lines to check what my companion had said.

In a post-study interview, this learner draws attention to the issue of messages being missed in busy areas of the game when many avatars congregated:

> I missed what other players said several times.

Another issue raised by a majority of learners was being ignored. In post-study interviews, several participants commented that although they made sustained efforts to communicate with higher-status players they were frequently ignored:

> In many cases, other players ignored me.
> They tend to just ignore you if you are low level.
> I felt those players who have long experience in the game don't want to talk with newcomers.

The above learners asserted that they found this situation to be frustrating. A design feature of the game may, in part, account for this finding. In their feedback, several learners noted that level restrictions created a situation where only players who had attained high status levels could communicate during certain game activities.

Although some learners expressed the view that the game was difficult to play other participants expressed a contrary view. One learner, who in the pre-study questionnaire claimed that they often play games, stated in a report that

> This game is not difficult to play, for there is a homepage which explains basic information in great detail.

Participants identified a number of areas where playing the game was beneficial. There was general agreement that playing the game improved language skills. In this context, one learner claimed that

> I improved my writing and reading skill by playing this game.

Several learners commented that playing the game helped them to respond more quickly and there were positive views expressed on the benefits of exposure to, and use of, the TL. In an interesting finding, that contradicts the questionnaire data, all but one of the participants claimed to have learned new vocabulary through playing the game. In a report, a learner expressed the general view that playing the game facilitated vocabulary learning stating that

> I learned many words and expressions during this game, especially while chatting with other players.

New vocabulary and usages identified by the learners included *double dealing, prestige, last but not least, invade, dote, break a leg, pollen,* and *put to good use.*
    The participants also identified other positive aspects of taking part in this research. They noted that it was beneficial and interesting to interact with players located in different countries, as may be observed in the following comments:

> Another good point is that you can communicate with many players from all over the world.
> It is very interesting to chat with people all over the world. I think it's a great merit of the game that it provides us with such an opportunity.

Participants further claimed that playing the game was enjoyable, as may be observed in the following statement that reflects the opinion of the majority:

> I can enjoy this game from the beginning.

This sentiment was noteworthy among the learners with higher proficiency levels. Several of these learners observed that the game became more challenging and fun to play as they progressed in level. In post-study feedback, a learner stated that

> As I leveled my character up during class, it got more and more enjoyable.

In post-study interviews, participants claimed that chatting in the game also increased their confidence and motivation:

> Another good point is that we can feel more confident about communicating with other players in English.
> I was motivated to learn English.

Several learners also expressed the opinion that playing the game was more interesting than taking part in a regular language class. The majority of participants claimed that although playing the game was challenging at times it was a useful experience. In written feedback regarding their overall experience learners made comments emphasizing positive aspects of participation in this research:

> I think it is helpful to study English.
> It was my first time to play the game in order to improve my English skills. I sometimes had difficulties, but it was an interesting experience.

Discussion

This case study was subject to a number of limitations. The number of participants was limited. Although the researcher had originally intended to schedule additional sessions and integrate them into a regular course this was not possible due to institutional constraints. Due to a scheduling issue, post-study feedback was only obtained from eight participants as two learners were unable in take part in the final session or complete the post-study questionnaire. Furthermore, the contradictory nature of some of the feedback draws attention to the limitations on learner self-reporting. These factors require acknowledgement in any attempt to generalize the findings to other contexts.

Although subject to limitations, this research provides a number of significant findings relevant to the research questions. A summary of key findings is provided in table 7.3.

Table 7.3   Significant findings on learner interaction and attitudes

Positive findings	Negative findings
Participation elicited the production of coherent TL output	TL output of variable quality
Exposure to new vocabulary	Negative attitudes expressed by the lower-level learners
Learners engaged in social interaction	Instances where technical issues hampered interaction
Learner participated in collaborative dialogue involving purposeful interaction in the TL	The specific game register presented challenges for the lower-level learners
Learners were highly engaged and took an active role in the interaction management	On occasion learners ignored by higher-status players
Learners established and maintained collaborative interpersonal relationships with other players	Instances of frustration
Motivation enhanced	
Instances of L1 use infrequent	
Self-correction	
Positive feedback from the majority of participants	

In answer to research question one, the data analysis confirms the results of prior research namely, that gameplay in a MMORPG elicits the production of TL output (Reinders and Wattana 2011). This study demonstrates that the participants engaged in forms of social interaction that are hypothesized as beneficial in social accounts of SLA. As table 7.3 shows, in a positive finding that mirrors previous work (Thorne 2008), analysis confirms that the learners engaged in collaborative dialogue involving purposeful interaction conducted almost entirely in the TL. Instances of L1 use were infrequent. The data indicates that the learners appeared highly engaged, adopting an active rather than a passive role in the management of their interaction. Evidence for this conclusion is confirmed by researcher observation and by the fact that the majority of participants consistently displayed motivation and enthusiasm throughout this research. In an interesting finding, the majority of the learners, who were volunteers, completed all of the sessions. Only the two low-level learners failed to complete the final session. As has been observed previously, although the learners encountered various challenges, their level of comfort with the game appeared to increase as this research progressed. The transcription and observation data shows the learners were, for the most part, able to utilize the communication systems provided and manipulate their avatars. Moreover, they were able to follow instructions provided by non-player characters and actively participate in quests with other players. Although the quality of the learner TL output was variable, the data shows that the learners consistently produced coherent TL output and, on occasion, engaged in self-correction. Taken together this evidence draws attention to the value of providing learners with training.

The transcript and observation data indicates that the learners not only initiated and sustained interaction, they consistently engaged in behaviors associated with language development in social accounts of SLA. The analysis shows that across the sessions the learners made requests for assistance, displayed reciprocity, and used humor. They also effectively employed continuers designed to signal interest and enthusiasm. These behaviors coupled to engagement in off-quest social interaction and the appropriate use of politeness created a communication context conducive to social cohesion and the continuation of the interaction. Moreover, these behaviors were largely effective in preventing misunderstandings in the absence of social context cues. Repeated participation in these types of interaction further facilitated the establishment and maintenance of collaborative interpersonal relationships that enabled the learners to undertake quests.

Data collected on learner attitudes reveals a number of findings relevant to research question two. The analysis draws attention to interesting differences in learner attitudes toward participation in this research, which reflect differences in proficiency levels. The majority of the participants who were higher level appeared able for the most part to deal with the communication environment. However, the two lower-level learners reported that they found the game challenging and experienced persistent difficulties during the sessions. A consistent theme in the learner feedback was that technical problems such as occasional system failures, and difficulties in following rapidly scrolling messages in crowed areas of the game, hampered the interaction at times. These factors induced frustration on the part of some participants. Further significant issues noted in the transcript and feedback data include problems comprehending elements of the unique register used in the game, and on occasion, being ignored by higher-level players.

Learner feedback further identifies a number of positive aspects of participation in this research. The high-level learners who formed the majority of the participants were particularly enthusiastic. The consensus view among these learners was that playing the game provided a useful means to improve English skills. These learners claimed that reading and writing skills were enhanced. They appreciated the opportunities for language practice and noted the benefits of interaction with interlocutors based overseas. For this learner group, playing the game appeared to foster interest, confidence, enjoyment, and motivation. The feedback data also draws attention to evidence indicating that the learners were exposed to new vocabulary. This finding lends support to the assertion made in previous research that play in MMORPGS over an extended period may facilitate the acquisition of vocabulary (Rankin, Gold, and Gooch 2006). The positive feedback from the majority of learners highlights the benefits of implementing training before utilizing an advanced MMORPG.

This chapter investigated use of the web-based MMORPG *Wonderland* with EFL learners based in Japan. The findings highlight the challenges presented by the use of this type of game in CALL. They further indicate that the above game is a viable and potentially beneficial arena for projects involving intermediate-level EFL learners. In a significant finding, it was found that the game elicited extensive social interaction in the TL. The presence of this phenomenon across the data though not conclusive evidence for learning nonetheless represents an encouraging finding. The analysis conducted in this chapter shows that *Wonderland* provides exposure to a rich context for collaborative interaction. Moreover, the data draws attention to the valuable opportunities for authentic learner-centered language practice. Although this research is subject to limitations, the presence of social interaction involving collaboration suggests that MMORPGs are promising venues for CALL. The broadly positive findings emphasize the need for future studies that explore the potential of participation in MMORPG-based gaming as a means to facilitate language development through TL interaction.

CHAPTER 8

Conclusions and Future Directions

Computer Games and Language Learning: Potentialities and Issues

A central aim of this book has been to answer the following question: Is participation in computer gaming beneficial for language learners? As the critical investigation carried out in the previous chapters demonstrates, the bulk of existing research indicates that many types of computer games represent viable tools for CALL, and that participation in gaming appears beneficial with regard to certain aspects of language learning. The analysis of research and the findings of the case study reported earlier in this discussion draw attention to a number of benefits identified repeatedly in the literature involving the majority of game types. Researchers emphasize the positive effects of exposure to the TL and new vocabulary in projects involving commercial and purpose-built games in both institutional and informal out-of-school settings (Cheung and Harrison 1992; deHaan 2005; Johns and Wang 1999; G. Jones 1986; Palmberg 1988; Piirainen-Marsh and Tainio 2009; Miller and Hegelheimer 2006; Ranalli 2008; Rankin, Gold, and Gooch 2006). The opportunities to develop reading, writing, and conversation skills are widely perceived as beneficial (Coleman 2002; Higgins, Lawrie, and White 1999; Johns and Wang 1999; Legenhausen and Wolff 1990; Piper 1986). In the case of network-based games that provide for real-time interaction such as, for example, MMORPGs, and MUVEs that incorporate games, research indicates that the opportunities for purposeful and authentic communication with native speakers and peers offers a number of benefits. These include a context conducive to the production of TL output, development of intercultural skills, and potentially valuable practice in interaction management (Johnson 2007; Reinders and Wattana

2011). Research on network-based games designed for social interaction suggests the communication context provided facilitates types of learner-centered collaborative interaction associated with language development such as dialogue, negotiation of meaning, zones of proximal development, and language socialization (Liang 2011; Thorne 2008; Zheng et al. 2009).

A consistent theme in the literature is broadly positive learner feedback and attitudes (Anderson et al. 2008; Johnson 2007; G. Jones 1986; Stubbs 2003; Thorne 2008). Studies conducted across game types provide evidence confirming that for intermediate- and high-level learners playing computer games elicits active engagement and interest (Higgins, Lawrie, and White 1999; Legenhausen and Wolff 1990; Liang 2011; Rankin, Gold, and Gooch 2006). Research suggests that most games frequently engender high levels of motivation and enjoyment (Chen and Yang 2011; G. Jones 1986; Stubbs 2003). However, researchers emphasize that the above benefits are not guaranteed and draw attention to the key role played by the teacher in securing positive learning outcomes (Anderson et al. 2008). A common theme across studies involving a variety of games is that their use calls for careful preparation and needs analysis (Miller and Hegelheimer 2006; Ranalli 2008). Moreover, the integration of game-based activities in the wider curriculum is widely perceived as enhancing learning (Neville, Shelton, and McInnis 2009).

Although research on the use of computer games in CALL has produced a range of encouraging findings this body of work also highlights a number of challenges inherent in their use. The discussion in earlier chapters has shown the use of some network-based games such as, for example, MMORPGs, requires unrestricted access to the Internet and a modern computing infrastructure. As with other types of technological innovation, these requirements may represent considerable barriers to use in many educational contexts. Another challenge of utilizing computer games lies in the need for training. The importance of this factor is emphasized in the literature. Although many learners have computer skills and gaming experience, research draws attention to the need for training particularly in the use of complex games (Anderson et al. 2008; Culley, Mulford, and Milbury-Steen 1986; Neville, Shelton, and McInnis 2009). The previous discussion shows that although some games provide walkthroughs and other types of contextual support, novice learners can greatly benefit from participation in training. Current research indicates that this should include not only guidance relating to technical features such as, for example, interface management, but also, in the case of social games, orientations that focus on the unique cultures and communication norms operating in different game communities. Individual practitioners should also be aware that even if appropriate training is undertaken positive learning outcomes are not guaranteed. The role of the individual teacher in carefully selecting a game that is appropriate to learner needs and interests appears crucial. The literature shows that when selecting a computer game for use with learners, researchers would be well advised to take steps to minimize the risks of frustration, cognitive overload, negative attitudes, and in the case of advanced social games, negative reactions from more experienced players.

A further issue identified in the literature is the risk of exposure to limited game-specific registers. This finding, identified in early research, is echoed in more recent work involving network-based games (Piper 1986; Reinders and Wattana 2011). This phenomenon again draws attention to the important role of individual practitioners in game selection. As stated previously, positive learner attitudes are a consistent finding in the existing literature. However, the influence of novelty effects and the limitations on learner self-reporting require acknowledgement in any assessment of learner-based research that emphasizes potential benefits of computer gaming. Although recent work on network-based games has provided evidence of self and other-initiated correction the prevalence of errors is a consistent finding across studies (Culley, Mulford, and Milbury-Steen 1986; Higgins, Lawrie, and White 1999; Reinders and Wattana 2011). The variable quality of the TL output reported in some studies draws attention to a factor emphasized in research, namely, the need for debriefing (Coleman 2002), and the important role played by the individual educator in facilitating the focus on the form necessary for language learning (Ellis 2005). As was noted at an earlier stage of this discussion, the careful integration of game activities into the regular curriculum and the provision of appropriate contextual supports offer an effective means to meet learner expectations and maximize the benefits of participation in computer gaming.

Computer Games and CALL: Paradigm Shift or False Dawn?

Answering the second question set out at the beginning of this book—does computer gaming represent, as has been claimed in relation to other spheres, a paradigm shift in language education?—is a challenging endeavor. Clearly the dramatic expansion in computer gaming that has occurred in recent years will increasingly influence all spheres of education including language education. However, at present it appears unlikely that a paradigm shift is about to occur. This book demonstrates the undoubted potential of certain types of computer games as tools for language learning. However, the analysis also draws attention to the limitations of current research and that evidence for learning is not yet conclusive. As has been emphasized in the literature, computer games are no panacea (Prensky 2001). In order for the potential of computer gaming to be fully realized, and for research to move forward, there is a need to avoid technocentrism and the view that the technological innovation can solve all of the many challenges faced by language educators. As the discussion in this book emphasizes, there is an unfortunate tendency among some CALL researchers to view the emergence of new technological innovations as potential breakthroughs. When the innovation in question fails to meet initial expectations or is rendered obsolete by the rapid pace of technological change development work is frequently abandoned. This leads to a situation where potentially valuable preliminary research is frequently not followed up, hindering systematic development work.

Although the recent expansion in the research base represents an important development, the limited number of studies coupled to the fact that computer games are not in widespread use in many institutional language learning contexts (Chik 2012) suggests that normalization in the sense proposed by Bax (2003, 2011) is, at present, far from being achieved. If significant long-term advances are to be made, then there is a need for a balanced and critical approach to development that acknowledges the potential of computer games and builds on prior research while also recognizing the challenges associated with their use. As has been argued previously, there is an urgent need for additional theory-led research as Reinders observes:

> The use of games needs to be informed by the principles and practice of second-language acquisition. (Reinders 2012, 7)

Fortunately, as this book shows, there is encouraging evidence in the contemporary literature of an increasing focus on theory-led development work that adopts the above approach (deHaan, Reed, and Kuwada 2010; Liang 2011; Piirainen-Marsh and Tainio 2009; Miller and Hegelheimer 2006; Ranalli 2008; Thorne 2008; Zheng et al. 2009). The following discussion explores some noteworthy contemporary development work involving a range of game genres that exemplifies this trend.

Contemporary Development Work

Zhao and Lai (2009) describe a browser-based MMORPG designed specifically for the study of Chinese as a foreign language. The design of this game known as *ZON* (http://enterzon.com/) draws on both cognitive and sociocultural SLA research as well as insights gained from computer game research. In order to create an authentic learning environment appropriate to learner needs the game is set in contemporary China. In an effort to motivate players a points system is adopted that is combined with character progression and content creation. Novice players are provided with a series of structured tasks designed to develop their character. In order to avoid issues with higher-status players, and to reduce anxiety, there is a newbie-friendly learning curve. New players start as tourists, and undertake a series of individual solo quests and interactions with game generated non-player characters that gradually become more challenging. On reaching a certain level in the game a player can then participate in interaction with other players. The game incorporates access to a range of quests that provide the individual player with exposure to rich TL input that is appropriate to proficiency level. This input reflects the TL culture and includes interactive multimedia objects and lessons. Players can access modeled conversations, and other forms of media such as Chinese language movies, radio broadcasts, TV shows, transcripts, cultural annotations, bulletin boards, and magazines. Quests model situations encountered in real life, such as renting an apartment, and are designed to elicit social interaction involving joint problem solving and discussion. They draw on authentic content with the goal of facilitating purposeful meaning-focused TL interaction, language socialization, and community building. The game further provides opportunities to focus on form, both during and after quests, through interaction with peers and native speaker players.

In a recent paper, Holden and Sykes (2011) report on the development and use of a place-based augmented reality game called *Mentira* (http://www.mentira.org/) designed for learning Spanish in a local neighborhood in the Southwestern United States. The design of the game draws on SLA and education research that emphasizes the social and situated nature of language learning. The game provides learners with opportunities to develop intercultural competence in a place-based context that is tied to the TL culture. *Mentira* uses a game engine designed for the iPod Touch and presents a fictional narrative revolving around events set in the prohibition era. The ultimate goal is for players is to solve a murder mystery set in the Los Griegos neighborhood of Albuquerque. In order to establish the identity of the murderer, players interact with and follow TL directions from non-player characters. During the gameplay, players explore various locations and collect clues tied to particular locations in Los Griegos. Each player is provided with different information and in order to solve the crime they must share clues with other players. The game is specifically designed for integration into a four-week-long Spanish course. During the course, the learners are first provided with an orientation and in subsequent weeks play three levels of the game in their free time. During this stage, the learners also go on a field trip. In the final week, the game acts as a stimulus for group work involving in-class discussions, debates, and voting.

Middlebury College in the United Sates has developed the online language program *MIDDWorld Online* (http://www.middleburyinteractive.com/products/) that incorporates a first person role-paying game designed to support the study of Spanish and French. The game design draws on sociocultural SLA research and presents players with opportunities to use the TL in authentic single and multiplayer simulations that model situations encountered in real life. Player controlled avatars are immersed in 3D virtual worlds that contain high quality renderings of cities modeled on locations found in the TL country. During gameplay learners of all levels of language proficiency can engage in a variety of quests that require social interaction in the TL with non-player characters and other players. Buildings in the game provide learners with access to a range of mini games. For example, in the café a player adopts the role of a waiter who must serve game-generated customers by using the TL appropriately and in a timely manner while at the same time maintaining high levels of customer satisfaction. In order to take multiple orders and engage in small talk, players drag and drop predesigned TL phrases into their avatars' speech bubble. If the correct phrase is selected the player gains satisfaction points. They then place the order in the correct category on the café order board. When the order is ready the player must serve it to the customer using the appropriate phrase. If during an interaction a player selects the wrong response they lose satisfaction points.

Sørensen and Meyer (2007) describe a web-based English learning environment *Mingoville* (http://www.mingoville.com/en.html) that incorporates games and is designed for children. The rationale for the game elements draws, in part, on SLA research that stresses the need to provide language learners with exposure to, and opportunities to use, the TL. Moreover, the environment is designed to provide a motivating context for meaningful and purposeful interaction that elicits communication and negotiation in the TL. A further influence on the design of *Mingoville* is serious game research. From this perspective, games are created not as mere entertainment, but for specific educational purposes. In this context, the games in *Mingoville* are designed to facilitate deep learning (Gee 2005) involving exploration, interaction, and play. The environment adopts a narrative whereby learners are immersed in a virtual city populated by English-speaking flamingoes. Each of the flamingoes has a unique personality. The English interface takes the form of a storybook that contains familiar characters found at home such as, for example, mothers and fathers and objects found in school including a textbook. The ten missions target specific language competences and curriculum goals and are based on distinct themes including, for example, family, animals, nature, sports, and media. Missions incorporate games that provide contextualized practice in using the TL such as vocabulary recognition and sentence construction.

Future Research

This chapter has focused on examining the potential benefits and issues associated with the use of computer games in CALL. The recent projects examined here highlight an encouraging trend, namely, the increasing influence of SLA research on the design of games used in CALL. As technology continues to advance and computer gaming becomes increasingly popular it has the potential to contribute significantly to the development of CALL and language education more generally in a manner substantially different from that in the past. In this context, research is likely to expand rapidly in the future. The discussion will now identify significant areas for future research.

In-Game Activities

As table 8.1 shows, the nature of the activities that learners undertake while playing computer games has been identified as a key issue in future research on the use of computer games in CALL (Reinhardt and Sykes 2012). As the discussion in this book confirms, although knowledge in this area is incomplete, there is sufficient evidence to indicate that not all games are appropriate for language learners. The review of the literature suggests that the cognitive demands presented by some genres such as, for example, rhythm games and sports games make them unsuitable for use in most language education contexts (deHaan 2005; deHaan, Reed, and Kuwada 2010). In addition, others types of games appear beneficial only when pedagogical supports are provided and they are used with learners who possess appropriate levels of language proficiency (Culley, Mulford, and Milbury-Steen 1986; Reinders and Wattana 2011). Moreover, although the opportunities for TL use provided by many games are widely viewed as valuable, this is in itself is no guarantee of learning as Thomas observes:

> It is clearly not satisfactory to argue that, merely because digital games involve use of the target language, that they are conducive to effective language learning (Thomas 2012, 26)

In this context, further research is necessary that systematically investigates the wide variety of commercial games currently available in order to identify

Table 8.1 Key areas and issues for investigation in future research

Area	Issue(s)
In-game activities	How can role-play be leveraged to enhance risk-taking? What aspects of communicative competence are facilitated by participation in network-based gaming? How can language socialization and cross-cultural knowledge be enhanced by participation in network-based gaming? What are the specific activities involved in learning elicited by different types of game?
Educator roles	How can games be effectively integrated into the regular curriculum? How can debriefing be utilized to maximize learning? What are teacher beliefs toward the use of computer games? What factors influence selection of particular game genres?
Modified games	How can modified games be used most effectively in CALL?
Gaming in informal contexts	What are the potential benefits of participation in gaming in informal out-of-school settings? How can insights gained from the investigation of gaming in informal contexts contribute to the creation of pedagogies and curricula that optimize the opportunities for learning provided by online gaming?
Learner variables	What is the role of affective factors? How do prior gaming experiences, training, and differences in proficiency level influence learning?

the most appropriate types for use with learners. This book draws attention to a number of genres that incorporate design features that provide contexts for learners to engage in activities and forms of interaction involved in language learning.

As has been stated at an earlier stage of this discussion, a number of different game types offer learners a range of activities that may facilitate aspects of language learning. Early research established that text-manipulation and adventure games can be motivating, provide useful language practice, and exposure to new vocabulary. As these games are widely available they continue to be investigated by researchers (Neville, Shelton, and McInnis 2009). To date, most work on the use of these games has been experimental and has involved small numbers of students. Although this has provided valuable insights at the micro level, there is a need for large-scale projects. Longitudinal studies involving significant numbers of learners offer the prospect of obtaining a broader perspective, as well as providing credible evidence confirming that the benefits identified in prior research can be realized in projects involving larger groups. The largely positive findings of research on the use of simulation games and MUVEs that contain games suggests that a similar approach would yield significant insights that would be of great value in shaping research and practice. The network-based nature of these games provides learners with access to new environments for learning that require further investigation. A potentially significant area of interest in future research may lie in exploring how role-play can be leveraged to encourage identity exploration, experimentation, and the risk-taking that plays an important role in language learning. Moreover, work that establishes the interactional patterns elicited offers the prospect of identifying the specific aspects of communicative competence that may be developed through participation in these games. Other areas with potential include research work that examines how the above games can be utilized to more effectively meet learner needs and studies that compare use of these games with other types of computer-based communication environment.

Of the contemporary computer games currently under investigation, MMORPGs have been identified as particularly promising arenas for CALL (Peterson 2010; Thorne, Black, and Sykes 2009). In this context, their use is attracting increasing interest from researchers. The quests found in these games structure interaction and incorporate features found in task-based learning (Thomas 2012). In a well-designed MMORPG players are immersed in an environment that requires them to undertake a series of goal-based activities. These become progressively more complex as players advance their characters in the game hierarchy. Although quests are challenging they are achievable through interaction with other players and non-player characters. Interaction with other players elicits participation in TL dialogue that frequently involves social interaction and the creation of collaborative interpersonal relationships. The peer feedback and scaffolding that is provided during this type of purposeful and meaning-focused interaction has been identified in interactionist SLA research as creating the conditions in which language acquisition may be facilitated. Furthermore, repeated participation in this type of interaction enhances motivation, and facilitates the creation of a low-risk context for communication. This context is conducive to language socialization and learning and may transfer to a formal learning environment if certain conditions are met, as Sykes, Reinhardt, and Thorne state:

> Multiplayer digital games are suitable for in-class task-based approach (Ellis 2003), if quests and various activities in the game are presented in a structure that focuses primarily on meaning exchange, and meets an instructional objective. (Sykes, Reinhardt, and Thorne 2010, 129)

The highly engaging contexts for TL use and social interaction created in MMORPGs make it likely that this type of game will be a major focus for future research. Longitudinal studies involving diverse learner groups that are conducted from the perspective of sociocultural SLA offer the prospect of revealing significant insights into aspects of learner behavior such as socialization, that are closely associated with language learning. The analysis of international projects may shed new light on the potential of participation in MMORPG-based gaming as a means to enhance cross-cultural knowledge and communicative competence. Moreover, there remains a need for studies that identify the specific activities involved in language learning engendered by participation in different types of game. Research in this area highlights the important role played by the individual practitioner in implementing CALL projects involving games and it is to an examination of this factor that the discussion now turns.

Educator Roles

An increasingly influential movement in education views the rise of computing technologies and the new forms of learning they make possible as a means to transform traditional educational systems and practices (Squire 2005). This perspective is highly critical of contemporary education and emphasizes that its key tenets, including standardization, high stakes testing, and a linier view of learning, are no longer appropriate for the new digital age (Prensky 2001; Shaffer et al. 2005). Much of the rhetoric associated with the use of Web 2.0 technologies and computer games in education emphasizes the opportunities technology provides to move away from teacher-dominated classrooms toward a learner-centered view of education (Osterweil and Klopfer 2012). This perspective has influenced practitioners and is reflected in CALL research on the use of games. Researchers cite the learner-centered nature of computer gaming coupled to the opportunities to develop autonomy as major justifications for its use (Chik 2011; García-Carbonell et al. 2001; Peterson 2010). Although this focus on the learner represents a welcome development the research analyzed in this book provides evidence that in formal educational contexts the individual educator has a key role to play in securing beneficial outcomes. Research indicates that active teacher intervention can greatly enhance learning when game projects are based on specific learner needs and are closely aligned with curricular goals. Moreover, regular participation in debriefing offers considerable benefits. Future research is needed that establishes the types of games that are most suitable for use in educational contexts. More studies that investigate how games can be more effectively integrated into the curriculum appear necessary, as does work that sheds new light into how debriefing can be utilized to maximize learning. Research conducted in these areas may yield important findings, as will studies that explore teacher beliefs toward computer games. Work that identifies the factors influencing the selection of particular games represents another potentially valuable avenue for future study.

Modified Games

The bulk of existing research on the use of computer games in CALL has involved commercial products. Although this work has produced encouraging findings, the literature shows that this approach is not without its problems. Research on the use of a variety of game types provides evidence that the steep learning curve provided by many advanced commercial games can hinder participation, particularly among learners who lack computer skills and appropriate gaming experience (Suh, S. Kim, and N. Kim 2010). Furthermore, the research reported in this book indicates that the registers used by high-status players in some commercial games may be problematic. This finding lends support to claims made in other studies that in order to maximize the benefits of participation in computer gaming game content should closely align with learner interests and needs (Anderson et al. 2008; Chen and Yang 2011). The modification of games to create environments designed specifically for language learning represents a significant trend in contemporary research. As the prior discussion shows, research on the use of a modified version of a commercial MMORPG run on a private server undertaken by Reinders and Wattana (2011) reported encouraging findings. The above researchers investigated the use of quests that required collaboration and purposeful use of the TL. These were aligned closely to learner proficiency level and were integrated into a regular language course. The researchers found that although the quality of learner TL output was variable, learner anxiety was reduced and willingness to communicate was enhanced. The promising findings of this study draw attention to the need for additional research that explores the potential of modified games. As this area is currently under-researched, more work is required in order to establish the most effective use of these games. Important areas of interest in future research may include investigations focusing on the role of narrative in shaping player experiences and the design of feedback. In the case of this latter factor, research on how failure states can be used to enhance learning represents an area rich in potential (Neville 2010). Another important issue that requires acknowledgement by CALL researchers is that computer gaming occurs largely outside the confines of formal educational contexts. An exploration of this phenomenon and its implications for future research is the focus of the following discussion.

Gaming in Informal Contexts

The rise of the Internet and Web 2.0 technologies has led to a dramatic worldwide expansion in the use of technology-mediated communication tools. These technologies are now widespread and have created a variety of new environments for human communication (Gee 2007b). As has been noted in the literature, these environments are frequently international, large scale, and informal in nature (Thorne, Black, and Sykes 2009). Moreover, many web-based communication environments operate outside traditional institutional contexts and use English as the default language (Sykes, Oskoz, and Thorne 2008). The potential of these environments to facilitate L2 use and development has been emphasized by CALL researchers. In the view of some researchers, participation in informal network-based computer gaming is potentially beneficial as it offers authentic opportunities for learning where the TL language is used as a resource for communication and socialization (Thorne, Black, and Sykes 2009). From this perspective, this type of gaming offers a means to move beyond the limitations of conventional language classrooms and engage learner groups that are frequently marginalized in traditional education (Thorne 2008). The emergence of this phenomenon offers opportunities for research into the new forms of L2 interaction, socialization, and development made possible by rapid advances in communication and gaming technologies. As participation in network-based gaming is now a widespread leisure time activity language learners are engaging in this form of activity in increasing numbers (Chik 2012). The literature suggests that this phenomenon is highly significant and that research at present is limited (Benson and Chik 2010; Piirainen-Marsh and Tainio 2009; Reinders 2012). The bulk of existing research on Internet-based gaming has been conducted in institutional settings and has involved learners based in North America and Europe. Further research is urgently required that investigates the potential of participation in gaming in informal out-of-school settings, as is work that focuses on learner groups located in diverse geographical locations. Studies on gaming that occurs outside of conventional educational contexts offer the prospect of providing significant new insights into how language development may occur in these environments. Future work on out-of-school gaming also has the potential to contribute to the creation of pedagogies and curricula that optimize the opportunities for learning provided by online gaming.

Learner Variables

The research analyzed in this book demonstrates the important influence of learner variables in CALL projects involving the use of computer games. Research draws attention to the important role played by affective factors such as attitudes, on learner participation and performance (Anderson et al. 2008; Rankin, Gold, and Gooch 2006). The majority of studies (G. Jones 1986; Liang 2011; Piirainen-Marsh and Tainio 2009; Stubbs 2003) confirm that playing a wide variety of computer games is frequently a motivating and enjoyable experience leading to broadly positive learner attitudes. These are frequently reported in studies involving games that provide real-time interaction and are appropriate to learner needs (Johnson 2007; Thorne 2008). Positive attitudes are also elicited when games are carefully integrated into regular courses (Miller and Hegelheimer 2006; Neville, Shelton, and McInnis 2009; Ranalli 2008; Reinders and Wattana 2011). However, participation in some types of games has been found to engender negative attitudes such as frustration and stress, particularly in games that require high degrees of skill, familiarity with specific game conventions, or frequent interaction with high-status players (Anderson et al. 2008; Chen and Yang 2011; Culley, Mulford, and Milbury-Steen 1986). Work has been conducted into learner attitudes toward a variety of games; although studies report broadly positive feedback they are not yet conclusive. More qualitative and quantitative work is needed into the role of affective factors. Furthermore, this book shows that a number of other important areas remain in need of additional research. The current body of research suggests that individual differences such as prior gaming experiences and proficiency level may greatly influence learner attitudes, performance, and participation (Suh, S. Kim, and N. Kim 2010). However, the influence of these factors remains poorly understood. To date, the majority of studies have focused on the use of games with intermediate- and advanced-level learners. More work is needed focusing on exploring the potential of a variety of game types for use with learners who possess lower levels of language proficiency. As was stated at an earlier stage of this discussion, learner training has repeatedly been identified in the literature as an important issue (Cheung and Harrison 1992; Coleman 2002). As training appears a key variable, additional research on the nature and role of learner training in projects utilizing advanced games may provide important insights of benefit in future research and practice.

The discussion conducted in this chapter demonstrates that computer gaming represents a significant phenomenon that has the potential to contribute greatly to the development of CALL. However, it has been shown that for the use of computer games to become widespread in formal educational contexts much additional theory-based research work is necessary. As has been noted in the discussion, such an approach provides a means to avoid technology-led development work and offers the added advantage of providing a robust and comprehensive framework for future research and practice. As computer gaming continues to expand, and interest in its use in education increases, researchers will doubtless explore new avenues in research focusing on both formal and informal contexts. This effort offers the prospect of revealing valuable new insights into the nature of technology-mediated language learning.

Bibliography

Aarseth, Espen. 2001. "Computer Game Studies, Year One." *Game Studies* 1 (1). http://www.gamestudies.org/0101/editorial.html.

Ahmad, Khurshid, Greville Corbet, Margaret Rogers, and Roland Sussex. 1985. *Computers, Language Learning and Language Teaching.* Cambridge: Cambridge University Press.

Anderson, Craig, and Brad Bushman. 2001. "Effects of Violent Video Games on Aggressive Behavior, Aggressive Cognition, Aggressive Affect, Physiological Arousal and Prosocial Behavior: A Meta-Analytic Review of the Scientific Literature." *Psychological Science* 12 (5): 353–359.

Anderson, Tom, Barry Lee Reynolds, Xiao-Ping Yeh, and Guan-Zhen Huang. 2008. "Video Games in the English as a Foreign Language Classroom." In *The Second IEEE International Conference on Digital Game and Intelligent Toy Enhanced Learning,* edited by Mike Eisenberg, Kinshuk, Maiga Chang, and Rory McGreal, 188–192. Los Alamitos, CA: IEEE Computer Society.

Andrews, Trish. 1994. "Videoconferencing: An Interactive Communication Tool for Distance Learners." *ON-CALL* 8 (2): 30–32.

Ang, Chee S. 2006. "Rules, Gameplay, and Narratives in Video Games." *Simulation & Gaming* 37 (3): 306–325.

Ang, Chee Siang., and Panayiotis Zaphiris. 2006. "Computer Games and Language Learning." In *Handbook of Research on Instructional Systems and Technology,* edited by Terry T. Kidd and Holim Song, 1–31. Hershey, PA: Information Science Reference.

Ariew, Robert. 1974. "Teaching French on PLATO IV." *System* 2 (1): 1–7.

Atkins, Barry. 2003. *More than a Game: The Computer Game as Fictional Form.* Manchester: Manchester University Press.

Atkinson, Dwight. 2002. "Toward a Sociocognitive Approach to Second Language Acquisition." *The Modern language Journal* 86 (4): 525–545.

Al-Seghayer, Khalid. 2001. "The Effect of Multimedia Annotation Modes on L2 Vocabulary Acquisition: A Comparative Study." *Language Learning & Technology* 5 (1): 202–232. http://llt.msu.edu/vol5num1/alseghayer/default.html.

Baltra, Armando. 1984. "An EFL Classroom in a Mystery House." *TESOL Newsletter* 18 (6): 15.

Bardovi-Harlig, Kathleen, and Zoltán Dörnyei. 2006. "Introduction to the Special Issue on Themes in SLA Research." *AILA Review* 19: 1–2.

Bartle, Richard. 2003. *Designing Virtual Worlds*. California: New Riders Publishing.

Bax, Stephen. 2003. "CALL-Past, Present, and Future." *System* 31 (1): 13–28.

———. 2011. "Normalization Revisited: The Effective Use of Technology in Language Education." *International Journal of Computer-Assisted Language Learning and Teaching* 1 (2): 1–15. doi:10.4018/ijcallt.2011040101.

Beatty, Ken. 2003. Teaching and Researching Computer-Assisted Language Learning. New York: Longman.

Benson, Phil, and Alice Chik. 2010. "New Literacies and Autonomy in Foreign Language Learning." In *Genre Theory and New Literacies: Applications to Autonomous Language Learning*, edited by María J. Luzón, Noelia Ruiz-Madrid, and María Luisa Villanueva, 63–80. Cambridge: Cambridge Scholars Press.

Berens, Kate, and Geoff Howard. 2001. *The Rough Guide to Videogaming 2002*. London and New York: Rough Guides.

Biber, Douglas. 1992. "Applied Linguistics and Computer Applications." In *Introduction to Applied Linguistics*, edited by Wiliam Grabe and Robert Kaplan, 257–278. Reading, MA: Addison-Wesley.

Bizzocchi, Jim. 2007. "Games and Narrative: An Analytical Framework." *Loading... The Journal of the Canadian Games Studies Association* 1 (1): 5–10. http://journals.sfu.ca/loading/index.php/loading/index/.

Blake, Robert. 1999. "Nuevos Destinos: A CD-ROM for Advanced Beginning Spanish." *CALICO Journal* 17 (1): 9–24.

———. 2000. "Computer Mediated Communication: A Window on L2 Spanish Interlanguage." *Language Learning & Technology* 4 (1): 120–136. http://llt.msu.edu/vol4num1/blake/default.html.

Brett, Paul. 1997. "A Comparative Study of the Effects of the Use of Multimedia on Listening Comprehension." *System* 25 (1): 39–53.

———. 1998. "Using Multimedia: A Descriptive Investigation of Incidental Language Learning." *Computer Assisted Language Learning* 11 (2): 179–200.

Brett, Paul, and M. Nash. 1999. "Multimedia Language Learning Courseware: A Design Solution to the Production of a Series of CD-ROMs." *Computers & Education* 32 (1): 19–33. doi.org/10.1016/S0360–1315(98)00038–4.

Bryce, Jo, and Jason Rutter. 2006. "An Introduction to Understanding Digital Games." In *Understanding Digital Games*, edited by Jo Bryce and Jason Rutter, 1–18. London: Sage.

Buckett, John, Gary Stringer, and Nac K. J. Datta. 1999. "Life After ReLaTe: Internet Videoconferencing's Growing Pains." In *CALL and the Learning Community*, edited by Keith Cameron, 31–38. Exeter, England: Elm Bank Publications.

Bulter-Pascoe, Mary Ellen. 2011. "The History of CALL: The Intertwining Paths of Technology and Second/Foreign Language Teaching." *International Journal of Computer-Assisted Language Learning and Teaching* 1 (1): 16–32. doi: 10.4018/ijcallt.2011010102.

Caillois, Roger. 1961. *Man, Play and Games*. New York: Free Press of Glencoe.

Chambers, Andrea, and Stephen Bax. 2006. "Making CALL Work: Towards Normalization." *System* 34 (4): 465–479.

Chapelle, Carol. 1997. "CALL in the Year 2000: Still in Search of Research Paradigms." *Language Learning & Technology* 1 (1): 19–43. http://llt.msu.edu/vol1num1/chapelle/default.html.

———. 1998. "Multimedia CALL: Lessons to Be Learned from Research on Instructed SLA." *Language Learning & Technology* 2 (1): 21–39. http://llt.msu.edu/vol2num1/article1/index.html.

———. 2004. "Technology and Second Language Learning: Expanding Methods and Agendas." *System* 32 (4): 593–601.

———. 2005. "Interactionist SLA Theory in CALL Research." In *CALL Research Perspectives*, edited by Joy Lynn Egbert and Gina Mikel Petrie, 53–64. New Jersey: Lawrence Erlbaum.

———. 2009. "The Relationship between Second Language Acquisition Theory and Computer-Assisted Language Learning." *The Modern Language Journal* 93 (1): 741–753.

Chapelle, Carol, and Patricia Duff. 2003. "Some Guidelines for Conducting Quantitative and Qualitative Research in TESOL." *TESOL Quarterly* 37 (1): 157–178.

Chapelle, Carol, and Joan Jamieson. 1981. "Language Lessons on the PLATO IV System." *System* 11 (1): 13–20.

Chen, Howard Hao-Jan, and Christine Yang. 2011. "Investigating the Effects of an Adventure Video Game on Foreign Language Learning." In *Proceedings of the 6th International Conference on E-learning and Games, Edutainment 2011*, edited by Maiga Chang, Wu-Yuin Hwang, Ming-Puu Chen, and Wolfgang Müller, 168–175. Berlin: Springer-Verlag.

Cheung, Anthony, and Colin Harrison. 1992. "Microcomputer Adventure Games and Second Language Acquisition: A Study of Hong Kong Tertiary Students." In *Computers in Applied Linguistics: An International Perspective*, edited by Martha Pennington and Vance Stevens, 155–178. Bristol: Multilingual Matters.

Chik, Alice. 2011. "Learner Autonomy Development through Digital Gameplay." *Digital Culture & Education* 3 (1): 30–44. http://www.digitalcultureandeducation.com/volume-3/learner-autonomy-development-through-digital-gameplay/.

———. 2012. "Digital Gameplay for Autonomous Foreign Language Learning: Gamers' and Language Teachers Perspectives." In *Digital Games in Language Learning and Teaching*, edited by Hayo Reinders, 95–114. New York: Palgrave Macmillan.

Chun, Dorothy M., and Jan L. Plass. 1996. "Effects of Multimedia Annotations on Vocabulary Acquisition." *The Modern Language Journal* 80 (2): 183–198.

Ciekanski, Maud, and Thierry Chanier. 2008. "Developing Online Multimodal Verbal Communication to Enhance the Writing Process in an Audio-Graphic Conferencing Environment." *ReCALL* 20 (2): 162–182.

Coiro, Julie 2003. "Reading Comprehension on the Internet: Expanding Our Understanding of Reading Comprehension to Encompass New Literacies." *The Reading Teacher* 56 (5): 458–464.

Cole, Peter, Robert Lebowitz, and Robert Hart. 1981. "A Computer Assisted Program for the Teaching of Modern Hebrew." *Studies in Language learning* 3 (1): 74–91.

Coleman, Douglas W. 2002. "On Foot in SIM CITY: Using SIM COPTER as the Basis for an ESL Writing Assignment." *Simulation & Gaming* 33 (2): 217–230.

Colpaert, Jozef. 2010. "Elicitation of Language Learners' Personal Goals as Design Concepts." *Innovation in Language Learning and Teaching* 4 (3): 259–274.

Cooke-Plagwitz, Jessamine. 2008. "New directions in CALL: An Objective Introduction to Second Life." *CALICO Journal* 25 (3): 547–557.

Crawford, Chris. 1984. *The Art of Computer Game Design*. Berkeley, CA: McGraw-Hill.

Csikszentmihalyi, Mihaly. 1990. *Flow: The Psychology of Optimal Experience*. New York: Harper & Row.

Culley, Gerald, George Mulford, and John Milbury-Steen. 1986. "A Foreign-Language Adventure Game: Progress Report on an Application of AI to Language Instruction." *CALICO Journal* 4 (2): 69–87.

Curtin, Constance, Douglas Clayton, Cheryl Finch, David Moor, and Lois Woodruff. 1972. "Teaching the Translation of Russian by Computer." *The Modern Language Journal* 56 (6): 354–360.

Darhower, Mark. 2002. "Interactional Features of Synchronous Computer-Mediated Communication in the Intermediate L2 class: A Sociocultural Case Study." *CALICO Journal* 19 (2): 249–276.

Davies, Graham. 1997. "Lessons from the Past, Lessons for the Future: 20 Years of CALL." In *New Technologies in Language Learning and Teaching*, edited by Ann-Karin Korsvold and Bernard Rüschoff, 27–52. Strasbourg: Council of Europe Publishing.

———. 2007. "Computer Assisted Language Learning: Where Are We Now and Where Are We Going?" Paper presented at the University of Warwick, England, October 3.

De Aguilera, Miguel, and Alfonso Mendiz. 2003. "Video Games and Education." *ACM Computers in Entertainment* 1 (1): 1–14.

deHaan, Jonathan. 2005. "Acquisition of Japanese as a Foreign Language through a Baseball Video Game." *Foreign Language Annals* 38 (2): 278–282.

deHaan, Jonathan, William M. Reed, and Katsuko Kuwada. 2010. "The Effect of Interactivity with a Music Video Game on Second Language Vocabulary Recall." *Language Learning & Technology* 14 (2): 74–94. http://llt.msu.edu/vol14num2/dehaanreedkuwada.pdf.

Dempsey, John V, Barbara A. Lucassen, Linda L. Haynes, and Maryann S. Casey. 1996. "Instructional Applications of Computer Games." Paper presented to the American Educational Research Association, New York, April 8–12.

DiCamilla, Frederick J., and Marta Anton. 2004. "Private Speech: A Study of Language for Thought in the Collaborative Interaction of Language Learners." *International Journal of Applied Linguistics* 14 (1): 36–69.

Donato, Richard. 1994. "Collective Scaffolding in Second Language Learning." In *Vygotskian Approaches to Second Language Research*, edited by James P. Lantolf and Gabriela Appel, 33–56. Norwood, NJ: Ablex.

Dondlinger, Mary Jo. 2007. "Educational Video Game Design: A Review of the Literature." *Journal of Applied Educational Technology* 4 (1): 21–31.

Dorval, Michel, and Michel Pépin. 1986. "Effect of Playing a Video Game on a Measure of Spatial Visualization." *Perceptual Motor Skills* 62 (1): 159–162.

Doughty, Catherine J. 1987. "Relating Second-Language Acquisition Theory to CALL Research and Application." In *Modern Media in Foreign Language Education: Theory and Implementation*, edited by William. F. Smith, 133–167. Lincolnwood, IL: National Textbook Company.

Duff, Patricia A. 2007. "Second Language Socialization as Sociocultural Theory: Insights and Issues." *Language Teaching* 40 (4): 309–319.

Dulay, Heidi, and Marina Burt. 1974. "Natural Sequences in Child Second Language Acquisition." *Language Learning* 24 (1): 37–53.

Eastment, David. 1996. "Survey Review: CD-ROM Materials for English Language Teaching." *ELT Journal* 50 (1): 69–79.

Egbert, Joy. 2005. "Conducting Research on CALL." In *CALL Research Perspectives*, edited by Joy Egbert and Gina M. Petrie, 3–8. New Jersey: Lawrence Erlbaum.

Egbert, Joy, Trena M. Paulus, and Yoko Nakamichi. 2002. "The Impact of CALL Instruction on Classroom Computer Use: A Foundation for Rethinking Technology in Teacher Education." *Language Learning & Technology* 6 (3): 108–126. http://llt.msu.edu/vol6num3/egbert/default.html.

Ellis, Rod. 1984. *Classroom Second Language Development: A Study of Classroom Interaction and Language Acquisition*. Oxford, UK: Pergamon.

———. 2003. *Task-Based Language Learning and Teaching*. Oxford, UK: Oxford University Press.

———. 2005. "Principles of Instructed Language Learning." *System* 33 (2): 209–224.

Eskelinen, Markku. 2001. "The Gaming Situation." *Game Studies* 1 (1). http://www.gamestudies.org/0101/eskelinen/.

Fabricatore, Carlo. 2000. "Learning and Videogames: An Unexploited Synergy." http://www.learndev.org/dl/FabricatoreAECT2000.PDF.

Felix, Uschi. 2000. "The Potential of CD-ROM Technology for Integrating Language and Literature: Student Perceptions." *German as a Foreign Language* 2: 48–63.

———. 2005. "Analyzing Recent CALL Effectiveness Research? Towards a Common Agenda." *Computer Assisted Language Learning* 18 (1–2): 1–32.

Fernández Carballo-Calero, Maria V. 2001. "The EFL Teacher and the Introduction of Multimedia in the Classroom." *Computer Assisted Language Learning* 14 (1): 3–14.

Fernandez-Garcia, Marasol, and Asuncion Martinez-Arbelaiz. 2002. "Negotiation of Meaning in Nonnative Speaker-Nonnative Speaker Synchronous Discussions." *CALICO Journal* 19 (2): 279–294.

Firth, Alan, and Johannes Wagner. 2007. "On Discourse, Communication, and (Some) Fundamental Concepts in SLA Research." *The Modern Language Journal* 91 (5): 757–772.

Fleta, Begoña M., Carmen P. Sabater, Luz G. Salom, Cristina P. Guillot, Carmen S. Monreal, and Edmund Turney. 1999. "Evaluating Multimedia Programs in Language Learning: A Case Study." *ReCALL* 11 (3): 50–57.

Foster, Pauline. 1998. "A Classroom Perspective on the Negotiation of Meaning." *Applied Linguistics* 19 (1): 1–23.

Foster, Pauline, and Amy S. Ohta. 2005. "Negotiation for Meaning and Peer Assistance in Second Language Classrooms." *Applied Linguistics* 26 (3): 402–430.

Fotos, Sandra S. 1993. "Consciousness Raising and Noticing through Focus on Form: Grammar Task Performance versus Formal Instruction." *Applied Linguistics* 14 (4): 385–407.

Frasca, Gonzalo. 1999. "Ludology Meets Narratology: Similitude and Differences Between (Video)games and Narrative. *Parnasso* 3: 365–371.

———. 2001. "Videogames of the Oppressed: Videogames as a Means for Critical Thinking and Debate." Masters thesis, Georgia Institute of Technology. http://www.ludology.org/articles/thesis/FrascaThesisVideogames.pdf.

———. 2003. "Simulation versus Narrative: Introduction to Ludology." In *The Video Game Theory Reader*, edited by Mark J. P. Wolf and Bernard Perron, 221–236. London: Routledge.

García-Carbonell, Amparo, Beverly Rising, Begoña Montero, and Frances Watts. 2001. "Simulation/Gaming and the Acquisition of Communicative Competence in Another Language." *Simulation & Gaming* 32 (4): 481–491.

Garrett, Nina. 1991. "Technology in the Service of Language Learning: Trends and Issues." *The Modern Language Journal* 75 (s1): 74–101.

———. 2009. "Computer-Assisted Language Learning Trends and Issues Revisited: Integrating Innovation." *The Modern Language Journal* 93 (s1): 719–740.

Gass, Susan M., and Evangeline A. Varonis. 1994. "Input, Interaction, and Second Language Production." *Studies in Second Language Acquisition* 16 (3): 283–302.

Gee, James P. 1992. *The Social Mind: Language, Ideology and Social Practice*. New York: Bergin and Garvey.

———. 1996. *Social Linguistics and Literacies: Ideology in Discourses*. London: Taylor Frances.

———. 1999. *An Introduction to Discourse Analysis: Theory and Method*. New York: Routledge & Kegan Paul.

———. 2003. *What Video Games Have to Teach Us about Learning and Literacy*. New York: Palgrave Macmillan.

———. 2005. "Learning by Design: Good Video Games as Learning Machines." *E-Learning* 2 (1): 5–16.

———. 2007a. "Are Video Games Good for Learning?" *Curriculum Leadership* 5 (1). http://cmslive.curriculum.edu.au/leader/default.asp?id=16866&issueID =10696.

———. 2007b. *What Video Games Have to Teach Us about Learning and Literacy*. 2nd ed. New York: Palgrave Macmillan.

———. 2009a. "Digital Media as an Emerging Field: Part 1; How We Got Here." *International Journal of Learning and Media* 1 (2): 13–23. http://www.mitpress-journals.org/toc/ijlm/1/2.

———. 2009b. "Digital Media as an Emerging Field: Part II; A Proposal For How to Use 'Worked Examples' to Move Forward." *International Journal of Learning and Media* 1 (2). http://www.mitpressjournals.org/toc/ijlm/1/2.

———. 2011. "Why Are Video Games Good for learning?" University of Wisconsin. Accessed January 11, 2012 http://www.academiccolab.org/resources/documents /MacArthur.pdf.

Gerber, Hannah P. 2009. "From the FPS to the RPG: Using Video Games to Encourage Reading YAL." *The ALAN Review* 36 (3): 87–91.

Goodfellow, Robin, Ingrid Jeffreys, Terry Milest, and Tim Shirra. 1996. "Face-to-Face Language Learning at a Distance? A Study of a Videoconference Try-Out." *ReCALL* 8 (2): 5–16.

Greenfield, Patricia M. 1984. *Mind and Media: The Effects of Television, Video Games, and Computers.* Harvard: Harvard University Press.

Gregg, Kevin R. 1993. "Taking Explanation Seriously; Or, Let a Couple of Flowers Bloom." *Applied Linguistics* 14 (3): 276–294.

Griffiths, Mark D. 1996. "Computer Game Playing in Children and Adolescents: A Review of the Literature." In *Electronic Children: How Children Are Responding to the Information Revolution*, edited by Tim Gill, 41–58. London: National Children's Bureau.

Grundlehner, Philip. 1974. "PLATO: German Reading, English as a Second Language, and Bilingual Education." *System* 2 (2): 69–76.

Gutierrez, Gabriela A. G. 2003. "Beyond Interaction: The Study of Collaborative Activity in Computer-Mediated Tasks." *ReCALL* 15 (1): 94–112.

Hagen, Stephen. 1995. "User Preferences in Open and Distance Language Learning: What are the Options for Multimedia?" *ReCALL* 7 (1): 20–25.

Hampel, Regine. 2003. "Theoretical Perspectives and New Practices in Audio-Graphic Conferencing for Language Learning." ReCALL 15 (1): 21–36.

Hampel, Regine, and Mirjam Hauck. 2004. "Towards An Effective Use of Audio Conferencing in Distance Language Courses." *Language Learning & Technology* 8 (1): 66–82. http://llt.msu.edu/vol8num1/hampel/default.html.

Harris, Jessica. 2001. "The Effects of Computer Games on Young Children—A Review of the research." RDS Occasional Paper No. 72. Research, Development and Statistics Directorate, Communications Development Unit, Home Office, London. http://library.npia.police.uk/docs/homisc/occ72-compgames.pdf.

Hart, Robert S. 1981. "The PLATO System and Language Study." *Studies in Language Learning* 3 (1): 1–24.

———. 1995. "The Illinois PLATO Foreign Languages Project." *CALICO Journal* 12 (4): 15–37.

Hart, Robert S., and Nolen Provenzano. 1973. *Russian Concentration*, Microfilm. Urbana, IL: University of Illinois

Hayes, Cynthia A., and Jan R. Holmevik. 2001. *High Wired: On the Design, Use and Theory of Educational MOOs.* Michigan: The University of Michigan Press.

Hays, Robert T. 2005. *The Effectiveness of Instructional Games: A Literature Review and Discussion.* Technical Report No. 2005–004. Orlando, FL: Naval Air Warfare Center Training Systems Division. http://www.dtic.mil/cgi-bin/GetTRDoc?AD =ADA441935%26Location.

Hewer, Sue. 1997. *Text Manipulation: Computer-Based Activities to Improve Knowledge and Use of the Target Language.* London: CILT.

Higgins, John, and Tim Johns. 1984. *Computers in Language Learning.* London: Collins.

Higgins, John, Ann M. Lawrie, and A. Goodith White. 1999. "Recognising Coherence: The Use of a Text Game to Measure and Reinforce Awareness of Coherence in Text." *System* 27 (3): 339–349.

Hlas, Anne C., and Monica Vuksanovic. 2007. "Computer Assisted Language Learning in Spanish Elementary School Foreign Language Classrooms: The Role of CD-ROMs." *Hispania* 90 (4): 769–783.

Holden, Christopher L., and Julie M. Sykes. 2011. "Leveraging Mobile Games for Place-Based Learning Language Learning." *International Journal of Game-Based Learning* 1 (2): 1–18. doi: 10.4018/978–1–4666–1864–0.ch003.

Hubbard, Philip. 1991. "Evaluating Computer Games for Language Learning." *Simulation and Gaming* 22 (2): 220–223.

———. 2009. *Computer-Assisted Language Learning: Critical Concepts in Linguistics.* London: Routledge.

Huh, Keun, and Wen-Chi Hu. 2005. "Criteria for Effective CALL research." In *CALL Research Perspectives,* edited by Joy L. Egbert and Gina M. Petrie, 9–21. New Jersey: Lawrence Erlbaum.

Huizinga, Johan. 1955. *Homo Ludens: A Study of the Play-Element in Culture.* Boston: Beacon Press.

Hutchins, Edwin. 1995. *Cognition in the Wild.* Cambridge, MA: MIT Press.

Ioannou-Georgiou, Sophie. 2006. "The Future of CALL." *ELT Journal* 60 (4): 382–384.

Iwabuchi, Takashi, and Sandra Fotos. 2004. "Creating Course Specific CD-ROMs for Interactive Language Learning." In *New perspectives on CALL for Second Language Classrooms,* edited by Sandra Fotos and Charles M. Browne, 149–168. New Jersey: Lawrence Erlbaum.

Jauregi, Kristi, and Emerita Bañados. 2008. "Virtual Interaction through Video-Web Communication: A Step towards Enriching and Internationalizing Language Learning Programs." *ReCALL* 20 (2): 183–207.

Jenkins, Henry. 2003. "Transmedia Storytelling." *MIT Technology Review.* http://www.technologyreview.com/news/401760/transmedia-storytelling/.

Jenkins, Henry. 2006. *Fans, Bloggers and Gamers: Exploring Participatory Culture.* New York: New York University Press.

Jepson, Kevin. 2005. "Conversations-and Negotiated Interaction-in Text and Voice Chat Rooms." *Language Learning & Technology* 9 (3): 79–98. http://llt.msu.edu /vol9num3/jepson/default.html.

Johns, Tim, and Lixun Wang. 1999. "Four Versions of a Sentence-Shuffling Program." *System* 27 (3): 329–338.

Johnson, L. Lewis. 2007. "Serious Use of a Serious Game For Language Learning." In *Proceedings of the 2007 Conference on Artificial Intelligence in Education: Building Technology Rich Contexts that Work,* edited by Rosemary Luckin, Kenneth R. Koedinger, and Jim Greer, 64–74. Amsterdam: IOS Press.

Jones, Christopher. 1986. "It's Not So Much the Program, More What You Do with It: The Importance of Methodology in CALL." *System* 14 (2): 171–178.

Jones, Glyn. 1986. "Computer Simulations in Language Teaching-the Kingdom Experiment." *System* 14 (2): 179–186.

Juul, Jesper. 2005. *Half Real: Video Games between Rules and Fictional Worlds.* Cambridge, MA: MIT Press.

Kasper, Gabriele. 1997. "'A' Stands for Acquisition: A Response to Firth and Wagner." *The Modern Language Journal* 81 (3): 307–312.

Kerth, Thomas. 1995. "Four Decades of CALL: A Collected Bibliography." In *Thirty Years of Computer Assisted Instruction: Festschrift for John R. Russell,* edited by Ruth H. Sanders, 144–154. Durham, NC: CALICO.

Kessler, Greg. 2007. "Formal and Informal CALL Preparation and Teacher Attitude Towards Technology." *Computer Assisted Language Learning* 20 (2): 173–188.

Kim, Hoe K. 2011. "Promoting Communities of Practice among Non-Native Speakers of English in Online Sessions." *Computer Assisted Language Learning* 24 (4): 353–370.

Kirriemuir, John, and Angela McFarlane. 2004. *Literature Review in Games and Learning: Report 8.* Bristol, England: Futurelab.

Kist, William. 2004. *New Literacies in Action: Teaching and Learning in Multiple Media.* New York: Teachers College Press.

Kohn, Kurt. 1995. "Perspectives on Computer Assisted Language Learning." *ReCALL* 7 (2): 5–19.

Koster, Raph. 2005. *A Theory of Fun for Game Design.* Scottsdale, AZ: Paragylph Press.

Kötter, Markus. 2003. "Negotiation of Meaning and Codeswitching in Online Tandems." *Language Learning & Technology* 7 (2): 145–172. http://llt.msu.edu/vol7num2/kotter/default.html.

Krashen, Stephen D. 1977. "The Monitor Model for Adult Second Language Performance." In *Viewpoints on English as a Second Language,* edited by Marina K. Burt, Heidi Dulay, and Mary B. Finocchiaro, 152–161. New York: Regents.

———. 1981. *Second Language Acquisition and Second Language Learning.* London: Pergamon Press.

———. 1982. *Principles and Practice in Second Language Acquisition.* New York: Pergamon Press.

———. 1985. *The Input Hypothesis: Issues and Implications.* New York: Longman.

———. 2003. *Explorations in Language Acquisition and Use.* Portsmouth: Heinemann.

Kress, Gunther. 2003. *Literacy in the New Media Age.* London: Routledge.

Künzel, Sebstian. 1995. "Processors Processing: Learning Theory and CALL." *CALICO Journal* 12 (4): 106–113.

Lafford, Barbara A. 2007. "Second Language Acquisition Reconceptualized? The Impact of Firth and Wagner (1997)." *The Modern Language Journal* 91 (s1): 735–756.

Lam, Yvonne. 2000. "Technophilia vs. Technophobia: A Preliminary Look at Why Second Language Teachers Do or Do Not Use Technology in Their Classrooms." *The Canadian Modern Language Review* 56 (3): 390–420.

Lankshear, Colin. 1997. *Changing Literacies.* Buckingham, UK: Open University Press.

Lankshear, Colin, and Michele Knobel. 2006. *New Literacies: Everyday Practices & Classroom Learning*. New York: Open University Press and McGraw Hill.

Lantolf, James P. 2000. "Second Language Learning as a Mediated Process." *Language Learning* 33 (2): 79–96.

Lantolf, James P., and Gabriela Appel. 1994. "Theoretical Framework: An Introduction to Vygotskian Perspectives on Second Language Research." In *Vygotskian Approaches to Second Language Research*, edited by James P. Lantolf and Gabriela Appel, 1–32. Norwood, NJ: Ablex.

Lantolf, James P., and Steven L. Thorne. 2006. "Sociocultural Theory and Second Language Acquisition." In *Theories in Second Language Acquisition*, edited by Bill Van Patten and Jessica Williams, 201–224. Mahwah, NJ: Erlbaum.

Larsen-Freeman, Diane, and Michael H. Long. 1991. *An Introduction to Second Language Acquisition Research*. London: Longman.

Laurel, Brenda. 1991. *Computers as Theater*. Menio Park, CA: Addison Wesley.

Lave, Jean. 1988. *Cognition in Practice: Mind, Mathematics, and Culture in Everyday Life*. Cambridge, UK: Cambridge University Press.

Lave, Jean, and Etienne Wenger. 1991. *Situated Learning: Legitimate Peripheral Participation*. Cambridge, UK: Cambridge University Press.

Lee, Lina. 2008. "Focus-on-Form Through Collaborative Scaffolding in Expert-to-Novice Online Interaction." *Language Learning & Technology* 12 (3): 53–72. http://llt.msu.edu/vol12num3/lee.pdf.

Legenhausen, Lienhard, and Dieter Wolff. 1990. "CALL in Use-Use of CALL: Evaluating CALL Software." *System* 18 (1): 1–13.

Leu, Donald J. 2001. "Internet Project; Preparing Students for New Literacies in a Global Village." *The Reading Teacher* 54 (6): 568–572.

Levy, Michael. 1997. *Computer Assisted Language Learning: Concept and Conceptualization*. Oxford: Oxford University Press.

———. 2000. "Scope, Goals and Methods in CALL Research: Questions of Coherence and Autonomy." *ReCALL* 12 (2): 170–195.

Levy, Michael, and Glenn Stockwell. 2006. *CALL Dimensions: Options and Issues in Computer-Assisted Language Learning*. New Jersey: Lawrence Erlbaum Associates.

Li, Rong-Chan, and David Topolewski. 2002. "ZIP & TERRY: A New Attempt at Designing Language Learning Simulation." *Simulation & Gaming* 33 (2): 181–186.

Liang, Mei-Ya. 2011. "Foreign Ludicity in Online Role-Playing Games." *Computer Assisted Language Learning* 25 (5): 455–469.

Lomicka, Lara L. 1998. "'To Gloss or Not to Gloss': An Investigation of Reading Comprehension Online." *Language Learning & Technology* 1 (2): 41–50. http://llt.msu.edu/vol1num2/article2/default.html.

Long, Michael H. 1985. "Input and Second Language Acquisition Theory." In *Input in Second Language Acquisition*, edited by Susan. M. Gass and Carolyn G. Madden, 377–393. Rowley, MA: Newbury House.

———. 1990. "The Least a Second Language Acquisition Theory Needs to Explain." *TESOL Quarterly* 24 (4): 649–666.

————. 1996. "The Role of the Linguistic Environment in Second Language Acquisition." In *Handbook of Second Language Acquisition*, edited by William C. Ritchie and Tej K. Bhatia, 413–468. San Diego: Academic Press.

————. 1997. "Construct Validity in SLA Research: A Response to Firth and Wagner." *The Modern Language Journal* 81 (3): 318–323.

Maftoon, Parviz, and Amin Shahini. 2012. "CALL Normalization: A Survey on Inhibitive Factors." *Jaltcall Journal* 8 (1): 17–32.

Malone, Thomas W. 1981. "Toward a Theory of Intrinsically Motivating Instruction." *Cognitive Science* 5 (4): 333–369.

Marty, Fernand. 1981. "Reflections on the Use of Computers in Second Language Acquisition-I." *System* 9 (2): 85–98.

————. 1982. "Reflections on the Use of Computers in Second Language Acquisition- II." *System* 10 (1): 1–11.

McAndrew, Patrick, Sandra P. Foubister, and Terry Mayes. 1996. "Videoconferencing in a Language Learning Application." *Interacting with Computers* 8 (2): 207–217.

Merriam, Sharan B. 1998. *Case Study Research in Education: A Qualitative Approach.* London: Jossey-Bass Publishers.

Miller, Megan, and Volker Hegelheimer. 2006. "The SIMs Meets ESL Incorporating Authentic Computer Simulation Games into the Language Classroom." *Interactive Technology and Smart Education* 3 (4): 311–328.

Mitchell, Alice, and Carol Savill-Smith. 2004. *The Use of Computer and Video Games for Learning: A Review of the Literature.* Ultralab, Angela Ruskin University: Learning and Skills Development Agency. http://gmedia.glos.ac.uk/docs/books/computergames4learning.pdf.

Mitchell, Rosamund, and Florence Myles. 2004. *Second Language Learning Theories.* London: Hodder Arnold.

Molla, Steven R., Alton F. Sanders, and Ruth H. Sanders. 1988. "Artificial Intelligence in a German Adventure Game: Spion on PROLOG." *CALICO Journal* 6 (1): 9–24.

Mondada, Lorenza, and Simon P. Doehler. 2004. "Second Language Acquisition as Situated Practice: Task Accomplishment in the French Second Language Classroom." *Modern Language Journal* 88 (4): 501–518.

Moore, Zena, Betsy Morales, and Sheila Carel. 1998. "Technology and Teaching Culture: Results of a State Survey of Foreign Language Teachers." *CALICO Journal* 15 (1–3): 109–128.

Morrison, Donald M. 1984. "GAPPER: A Microcomputer-Based Learning Game." *System* 12 (2): 169–180.

Murray, Janet H. 1997. *Hamlet on the Holodeck: The Future of Narrative in Cyberspace.* New York: The Free Press.

Murray, Liam, and Ann Barnes. 1998. "Beyond the 'Wow' Factor-Evaluating Multimedia Software From a Pedagogical Viewpoint." *System* 26 (2): 249–259.

Neville, David O. 2010. "Structuring Narrative in 3D Digital Game-Based Learning Environments to Support Second Language Acquisition." *Foreign Language Annals* 43 (3): 446–469.

Neville, David O., Brett E. Shelton, and Brian McInnis. 2009. "Cybertext Redux: Using Digital Game-Based Learning to Teach L2 Vocabulary, Reading, and Culture." *Computer Assisted Language Learning* 22 (5): 409–424.

Newman, James. 2004. *Videogames*. London: Routledge.

Ochs, Elinor, and Bambi Schieffelin. 1995. "The Impact of Language Socialization on Grammatical Development." In *The Handbook of Child Language*, edited by Paul Fletcher and Brian MacWhinney, 73–94. Oxford: Blackwell.

O'Dowd, Robert. 2000. "Intercultural Learning via Videoconferencing: A Pilot Exchange Project." *ReCALL* 12 (1): 49–61.

Ohta, Amy S. 2000. "Rethinking Interaction in SLA: Developmentally Appropriate Assistance in the Zone of Proximal Development and the Acquisition of L2 Grammar." In *Sociocultural Theory and Second Language Learning* edited by James P. Lantolf, 51–78. Oxford: Oxford University Press.

O'Neil, Harold F., Richard Waitess, and Eva L. Baker. 2005. "Classification of Learning Outcomes: Evidence from the Computer Games Literature." *The Curriculum Journal* 16 (4): 455–474.

Osterweil, Scott, and Eric Klopfer. 2012. "All Games Are Child's Play?" In *Digital Games and Learning*, edited by Sarah de Freitas and Paul Maharg, 152–171. London: Continuum.

Oxford, Rebecca L. 1995. "Linking Theories of Learning with Intelligent Computer-Assisted Language Learning." In *Intelligent Language Tutors: Theory Shaping Technology*, edited by Melissa V. Hollland, Jonathan D. Kaplan, and Michelle R. Sams, 359–369. Mahwah, NJ: Lawrence Erlbaum.

Palmberg, Rolf. 1988. "Computer Games and Foreign-Language Vocabulary Learning." *ELT Journal* 42 (2): 247–252.

Perkins, Jan. 1999. "Problems in Telematics." In *Telematics in Education: Trends and Issues*, edited by Michelle Selinger and John Pearson, 1–14. Amsterdam: Pergamon.

Peterson, Mark. 2001. "MOOs and Second Language Acquisition: Towards a Rationale for MOO-Based Learning." *Computer Assisted Language Learning* 14 (5): 443–459.

———. 2010. "Massively Multiplayer Online Role-Playing Games as Arenas for Second Language Learning." *Computer Assisted Language Learning* 23 (5): 429–439.

———. 2011. "Towards a Research Agenda for the Use of Three-Dimensional Virtual Worlds in Language Learning." *CALICO Journal* 29 (1): 67–80.

Philips, Martin. 1987. "Potential Paradigms and Possible Problems for CALL." *System* 15 (3): 275–287.

Piaget, Jean. 1961. *Play, Dreams and Imitation in Childhood*. New York: Norton.

Pica, Teresa. 1994. "Research on Negotiation: What Does It Reveal about Second-Language Learning Conditions, Processes, and Outcomes?" *Language Learning* 44 (3): 493–527.

Pienemann, Manfred. 2007. "Processability Theory." In *Theories in Second Language Acquisition*, edited by Bill VanPatten and Jessica Williams, 137–154. Mahwah, NJ: Lawrence Erlbaum Associates.

Piirainen-Marsh, Arja, and Liisa Tainio. 2009. "Other-Repetition as a Resource for Participation in the Activity of Playing a Video Game." *The Modern Language Journal* 93 (2): 153–169.

Piper, Alison. 1986. "Conversation and the Computer: A Study of the Conversational Spin-Off Generated among Learners of English as a Foreign Language Working in Groups." *System* 14 (2): 187–198.

Plass, Jan L., Dorothy M. Chun, Richard E. Mayer, and Detlev Leutner. 1998. "Supporting Visual and Verbal Learning Preferences in a Second-Language Multimedia Learning Environment." *Journal of Educational Psychology* 90 (1): 25–36.

Plass, Jan L., and Linda C. Jones. 2005. "Multimedia Learning in Second Language Acquisition." In *The Cambridge Handbook of Multimedia*, edited by Richard E. Mayer, 467–468. Cambridge: Cambridge University Press.

Prensky, Marc. 2001. *Digital Game-Based Learning*. New York: McGraw-Hill.

———. 2002. "The Motivation of Gameplay: The Real Twenty-First Century Learning Revolution." *On the Horizon* 10 (1): 5–11. doi:10.1108/107481202 10431349.

———. 2006a. *Don't Bother Me Mom-I'm Learning*. Saint Paul, MN: Paragon House.

———. 2006b. "Listen to the Natives." *Educational Leadership* 63 (4): 8–13.

Ranalli, Jim. 2008. "Learning English with The Sims: Exploiting Authentic Computer Simulation Games for L2 Learning." *Computer Assisted Language Learning* 21 (5): 441–455.

Randel, Josephine M., Barbara A. Morris, C. Douglas Wetzel, and Betty V. Whitehill. 1992. "The Effectiveness of Games for Educational Purposes: A Review of Recent Research." *Simulation & Gaming* 23 (3): 261–276.

Rankin, Yolanda A., Rachel Gold, and Bruce Gooch. 2006. "3D Role-Playing Games as Language Learning Tools." In *Proceedings of EuroGraphics 2006*, edited by Eduard Gröller and László Szirmay-Kalos. New York: ACM.

Reinders, Hayo. 2012. "Introduction." In *Digital Games in Language Learning and Teaching*, edited by Hayo Reinders, 1–8. New York: Palgrave Macmillan.

Reinders, Hayo, and Sorada Wattana, S. 2011. "Learn English or Die: The Effects of Digital Games on Interaction and Willingness to Communicate in a Foreign Language." *Digital Education & Culture* 3 (1): 4–28. http://www.digitalculture andeducation.com/cms/wpcontent/uploads/2011/04/dce1049_reinders_2011 .pdf.

Reinhardt, Jonathon, and Julie M. Sykes. 2012. "Conceptualizing Digital Game-Mediated L2 Learning and Pedagogy: Game-Enhanced and Game-Based Research and Practice." In *Digital Games in Language Learning and Teaching*, edited by Hayo Reinders, 32–49. New York: Palgrave Macmillan.

Robinson, Peter. 1995. "Attention, Memory, and the 'Noticing' Hypothesis." *Language Learning* 45 (2): 283–331.

Ryan, Marie-Laure. 2002. "Beyond Myth and Metaphor: Narrative in Digital Media." *Poetics Today* 23 (4): 581–609.

———. 2006. *Avatars of Story*. Minnesota: University of Minnesota Press.

Salaberry, Rafael. 1999. "CALL in the Year 2000: Still Developing the Research Agenda." *Language Learning & Technology* 3 (1): 104–107. http://www.llt.msu .edu/vol3num1/comment/.

———. 2001. "The Use of Technology for Second Language Learning and Teaching: A Retrospective." *The Modern Language Journal* 85 (1): 39–56.

Salen, Katie. 2007. "Gaming Literacies: What Kids Learn through Design." *Journal of Educational Multimedia and Hypermedia* 16 (3): 301–322.

Salen, Katie, and Eric Zimmerman. 2004. *Rules of Play: Game Design Fundamentals.* Cambridge, MA : MIT Press.

Sanders, Ruth H. 1995. "Thirty Years of Computer-Assisted Language Instruction: Introduction." *CALICO Journal* 12 (4): 7–14.

Sanford, Kathy, and Leanna Madill. 2007. "Understanding the Power of New Literacies through Video Game Play and Design." *Canadian Journal of Education* 30 (2): 432–455.

Schmidt, Richard W. 1990. "The Role of Consciousness in Second Language Learning." *Applied Linguistics* 11 (2): 129–58.

———. 1992. "Awareness and Second Language Acquisition." *Annual Review of Applied Linguistics* 13: 206–226.

Shaffer, David W., Kurt R. Squire, Richard Halverson, and James P. Gee. 2005. "Video Games and the Future of Learning." *Phi Delta Kappan* 87 (2): 104–111.

Shin, Dong-Shin. 2006. "ESL Students Computer-Mediated Communication Practices: Context Configuration." *Language Learning & Technology* 10 (3): 65–84. http://llt.msu.edu/vol10num3/shin/default.html.

Silvern, Steven B. 1986. "Classroom Use of Videogames." *Educational Research Quarterly* 10 (1): 10–16.

Simons, Jan. 2007. "Narrative, Games and Theory." *International Journal of Computer Game Research* 7 (1). http://gamestudies.org/0701/articles/simons.

Skinner, Burrhus F. 1954. "The Science of Learning and the Art of Teaching." *Harvard Educational Review* 24 (2): 86–97.

———. 1957. *Verbal Behavior.* Acton, MA: Copley Publishing Group.

———. 1968. *The Technology of Teaching.* New York: Appleton Century Crofts.

Smith, Bryan. 2003. "Computer-Mediated Negotiated Interaction: An Expanded Model." *The Modern Language Journal* 87 (1): 38–57.

Sørensen, Birgitte H., and Bente Meyer. 2007. "Serious Games in Language Learning and Teaching—A Theoretical Perspective." In *Proceedings of the DiGRA 2007 Conference*, edited by Akira Baba, 559–566. Tokyo: Digital Games Research Association.

Squire, Kurt. 2005. "Changing the Game: What Happens When Video Games Enter the Classroom." *Innovate* 1 (6). http://innovateonline.info/pdf/vol1_issue6 /Changing_the_Game-__What_Happens_When_Video_Games_Enter_the _Classroom_.pdf.

———. 2011. *Video Games and Learning: Teaching and Participatory Culture in the Digital Age.* New York: Teachers College Press.

Squire, Kurt, and Henry Jenkins. 2003. "Harnessing the Power of Games in Education." *Insight* 3 (1): 5–33.

Steinkuehler, Constance A. 2004. "Learning in Massively Multiplayer Online Games." In *Embracing Diversity in the Learning Sciences: Proceedings of the Sixth International Conference of the Learning Sciences*, edited by Yasmin B. Kafai, William A. Sandoval, Noel Enyedy, Althea S. Nixon, and Francisco Herrera, 521–528. Mahwah, NJ: Lawrence Erlbaum Associates.

————. 2006. "Massively Multiplayer Online Videogaming as Participation in a Discourse." *Mind, Culture, & Activity* 13 (1): 38–52.

————. 2007. "Massively Multiplayer Online Gaming as a Constellation of Literacy Practices." *E-Learning* 4 (3): 297–318.

————. 2008a. "Cognition and Literacy in Massively Multiplayer Online Games." In *Handbook of Research on New Literacies*, edited by Julie Coiro, Michele Knobel, Colin Lankshear, and Donald J. Leu, 611–634. Mahwah, NJ: Lawrence Erlbaum Associates.

————. 2008b. "Massively Multiplayer Online Games as an Educational Technology: An Outline for Research." *Educational Technology* 48 (1):10–21.

Stockwell, Glenn. 2007. "A Review of Technology Choice for Teaching Language Skills in the CALL Literature." *ReCALL* 19 (2): 105–120.

Street, Brian. 2003. "What's New in New Literacy Studies?" *Current Issues in Comparative Education* 5 (2): 1–14.

Stubbs, Kristen. 2003. "Kana no Senshi (Kana Warrior): A New Interface for Learning Japanese Characters." Poster presented at the Conference on Human Factors and Computing Systems, Ft. Lauderdale, Florida, USA, April.

Suh, Soonshik, S. W. Kim, and N. J. Kim. 2010. "Effectiveness of MMORPG-Based Instruction in Elementary English Education in Korea." *Journal of Computer Assisted Learning* 26 (5): 370–378.

Sundqvist, Pia, and Liss K. Sylvén. 2012. "World of VocCraft: Computer Games and Swedish Learners' L2 English Vocabulary." In *Digital Games in Language Learning and Teaching*, edited by Hayo Reinders, 189–208. New York: Palgrave Macmillan.

Sutton-Smith, Brian. 2001. *The Ambiguity of Play*. Boston: Harvard University Press.

Swain, Merrill. 1985. "Communicative Competence: Some Roles of Comprehensible Input and Comprehensible Output in Its Development." In *Input in Second Language Acquisition*, edited by Susan M. Gass and Carolyn G. Madden, 235–253. Rowley, MA: Newbury House.

————. 1995. "Three Functions of Output in Second Language Learning." In *Principle and Practice in Applied Linguistics: Studies in Honour of H.G. Widdowson*, edited Guy Cook and Barbara Seidlhofer, 123–143. Oxford: Oxford University Press.

Swain, Merrill, and Ping Deters. 2007. "'New' Mainstream SLA Theory: Expanded and Enriched." *The Modern Language Journal* 91 (5): 820–836.

Swain, Merrill, and Sharon Lapkin. 1995. "Problems in Output and the Cognitive Processes They Generate: A Step Towards Second Language Learning." *Applied Linguistics* 16 (3): 371–391.

Sydorenko, Tetyana. 2010. "Modality of Input and Vocabulary Acquisition." *Language Learning & Technology* 14 (2): 50–73. http://llt.msu.edu/vol14num2/sydorenko.pdf.

Sykes, Julie M., Ana Oskoz, and Steven L. Thorne. 2008. "Web 2.0, Synthetic Immersive Environments, and Mobile Resources for Language Education." *CALICO Journal* 25 (3): 528–546.

Sykes, Julie M., Jonathon Reinhardt, and Steven L. Thorne. 2010. "Multiuser Digital Games as Sites for Research and Practice." In *Directions and Prospects Educational Linguistics*, edited by Frances M. Hult, 117–135. Amsterdam: Springer.

Tarone, Elaine. 2007. "Sociolinguistic Approaches to Second Language Acquisition Research." *The Modern Language Journal* 91 (s1): 837–848.

Thorne, Steven L. 2008. "Transcultural Communication in Open Internet Environments and Massively Multiplayer Online Games." In *Mediating Discourse Online*, edited by Sally S. Magnan, 305–327. Amsterdam: John Benjamins.

Thorne, Steven L., Rebecca W. Black, and Julie M. Sykes. 2009. "Second Language Use, Socialization, and Learning in Internet Interest Communities and Online Gaming." *The Modern Language Journal* 93 (s1): 802–821.

Thomas, Michael. 2012. "Contextualizing Digital Game-Based Language Learning: Transformational Paradigm Shift or Business as Usual?" In *Digital Games in Language Learning and Teaching*, edited by Hayo Reinders, 11–31. New York: Palgrave Macmillan.

Timuçin, Metin. 2006. "Implementing CALL in an EFL Context." *ELT Journal* 60 (3): 262–271.

Varonis, Evangeline M., and Susan Gass. 1985. "Non-Native/Non-Native Conversation: A Model for Negotiation of Meaning." *Applied Linguistics* 6 (1): 71–90.

Von Der Emde, Silke, Jeffrey Schneider, and Markus Kötter. 2001. "Technically Speaking: Transforming Language Learning through Virtual Learning Environments (MOOs)." *The Modern language Journal* 85 (2): 210–225.

Vygotsky, Lev S. 1978. *Mind in Society: The Development of Higher Psychological Processes*. Cambridge, MA: Harvard University Press.

Wang, Yuping. 2004. "Distance Language Learning: Interactivity and Fourth Generation Internet-Based Videoconferencing." *CALICO Journal* 21 (2): 373–395.

———. 2006. "Negotiation of Meaning in Desktop Videoconferencing-Supported Language Learning." *ReCALL* 18 (1): 122–146.

Warschauer, Mark. 1996. "Computer Assisted Language Learning: An Introduction." In *Multimedia Language Teaching*, edited by Sandra Fotos, 3–20. Tokyo: Logos International.

Warschauer, Mark, and Deborah Healey. 1998. "Computers and Language Learning: An Overview." *Language Teaching* 31 (2): 57–71.

Warschauer, Mark, and Richard Kern. 2000. "Theory and Practice of Network-Based Language Teaching." In *Network-Based Language Teaching: Concepts and Practice*, edited by Mark Warschauer and Richard Kern, 1–19. Cambridge: Cambridge University Press.

Warschauer, Mark, Lonnie Turbee, and Bruce Roberts. 1996. "Computer Learning Networks and Student Empowerment." *System* 24 (1): 1–14.

Watson-Gegeo, Karen Ann, and Sarah Nielsen. 2003. "Language Socialization in SLA." In *The Handbook of Second Language Acquisition*, edited by Catherine J. Doughty and Michael H. Long, 19–42. Malden, MA: Blackwell.

Watts, Noel. 1997. "A Learner-Based Design Model for Interactive Multimedia Language Learning Packages." *System* 25 (1): 1–8.

Wenger, Etienne. 1998. *Communities of Practice: Learning, Meaning, and Identity.* Cambridge: Cambridge University Press.

Wertsch, James V. 2007. "Mediation." In *The Cambridge Companion to Vygotsky,* edited by Harry Daniels, Michael Cole, and James V. Wertsch, 178–192. Cambridge: Cambridge University Press.

Whitton, Nicola. 2010. *Learning with Digital Games: A Practical Guide to Engaging Students in Higher Education.* New York: Routledge.

Wolf, Mark J. P., and Bernard Perron, B. 2003. "Introduction." In *The Video Game Theory Reader,* edited by Mark J. P. Wolf and Bernard Perron, 1–24. London: Routledge.

Wong, Jan, and Agnès Fauverge. 1999. "LEVERAGE—Reciprocal Peer Tutoring over Broadband Networks." *ReCALL* 11 (1): 33–142.

Woodbury, Verl. 1998. "CD-ROM: Potential and Practicalities." *CALICO Journal* 6 (1): 25–35.

Wouters, Pieter, Eric van der Spek, and Herre van Oostendorp. 2009. "Current Practices in Serious Game Research: A Review from a Learning Outcomes Perspective." In *Games-Based Learning Advancements for Multisensory Human Computer Interfaces: Techniques and Effective Practices,* edited by Thomas Connolly, Mark Stansfield, and Liz Boyle, 233–250. Hershey, PA: IGI Global.

Yanguas, Iñigo. 2009. "Multimedia Glosses and Their Effect on L2 Text Comprehension and Vocabulary Learning." *Language Learning & Technology* 13 (2): 48–67. http://llt.msu.edu/vol13num2/yanguas.pdf.

Yoshii, Makoto. 2006. "L1 and L2 Glosses: Their Effects on Incidental Vocabulary Learning." *Language Learning & Technology* 10 (3): 85–101. http://llt.msu.edu /vol10num3/pdf/yoshii.pdf.

Zähner, Christopher, Agnes Fauverge, and Jan Wong. 2000. "Task-based Language Learning via Audiovisual Networks: The LEVERAGE Project." In *Network-Based Language Teaching: Concepts and Practice,* edited by Mark Warschauer and Richard Kern, 186–203. Cambridge, England: Cambridge University Press.

Zagal, Jose P. 2010. *Ludoliteracy: Defining, Understanding, and Supporting Games Education.* Pittsburgh, PA: ETC Press.

Zhao, Yong, and Lai Chun. 2009. "MMORPGS and Foreign Language Education." In *Handbook of Research on Effective Electronic Gaming in Education,* edited by Richard E. Ferdig, 402–421. New York: IDEA Group.

Zheng, Dongping, Michael F. Young, Manuela M. Wagner, and Robert A. Brewer. 2009. "Negotiation for Action: English Language Learning in Game-Based Virtual Worlds." *The Modern Language Journal* 93 (4): 489–511.

Zuengler, Jane, and Elizabeth R. Miller. 2006. "Cognitive and Sociocultural Perspectives: Two Parallel SLA Worlds?" *TESOL Quarterly* 40 (1): 35–58.

Index

GPSR Compliance
The European Union's (EU) General Product Safety Regulation (GPSR) is a set
of rules that requires consumer products to be safe and our obligations to
ensure this.

If you have any concerns about our products, you can contact us on

ProductSafety@springernature.com

In case Publisher is established outside the EU, the EU authorized
representative is:

Springer Nature Customer Service Center GmbH
Europaplatz 3
69115 Heidelberg, Germany